Thomas Hardy's Shorter Fiction

Thomas Hardy's Shorter Fiction
A Critical Study

Sophie Gilmartin and Rod Mengham

Edinburgh University Press

© Sophie Gilmartin and Rod Mengham, 2007

Edinburgh University Press Ltd
22 George Square, Edinburgh

Typeset in Sabon and Futura
by Servis Filmsetting Ltd, Manchester, and
printed and bound in Great Britain by
Biddles Ltd, King's Lynn, Norfolk

A CIP record for this book is available from the British Library

ISBN 978 0 7486 3265 7 (hardback)

The right of Sophie Gilmartin and Rod Mengham
to be identified as authors of this work
has been asserted in accordance with
the Copyright, Designs and Patents Act 1988.

Contents

Preface — vii
Acknowledgements — xi
Textual Note — xii

1 *Wessex Tales* — 1
2 *A Group of Noble Dames* — 53
3 *Life's Little Ironies* — 93
4 *A Changed Man* — 117

Select Bibliography — 136
Index — 141

Preface

This compact study of Hardy's short stories provides detailed readings of many individual texts as well as giving an account of the ruling preoccupations and recurrent writing strategies of the entire corpus. It relates the formal choices imposed on Hardy as contributor to no fewer than twenty-four separate periodicals to the methods he employed to encode in fiction his troubled attitude towards the social and cultural politics of the West Country, where most of the stories are set. There is also a close examination of the extent to which the stories bring out, more pervasively than the novels, the problems of author/reader relations that reached a critical phase for Hardy in the 1890s. No previous study has shown how the powerful challenge to readerly competence mounted in the stories reveals the complexity of Hardy's motivations during a period when he was moving progressively in the direction of exchanging fiction for poetry.

It is partly because our study has an historical bearing that we have chosen to deal with the stories in chronological order of publication. But there is another, more compelling, rationale: a particular feature of Hardy's career as a short-story writer is the close relationship he establishes between many (not all) stories in each individual volume. Apart from the situation with *A Changed Man*, this reflects his practice of collecting into each volume material written within the same relatively short period of time; that chronological condensation often entails historical coherence of precisely the kind that our study is orientated towards.

Chapter 1 is concerned with *Wessex Tales*, whose stories provide vivid instances of the nature of Hardy's 'telescopic' vision, drawing attention to the wide and extended context of landscape in its temporal and spatial aspects, while also focusing in on the details of personal circumstance; combining awareness of both far and near, often counterpointing the evidence of marks on the landscape with that of marks on the body. This mediation between what seems most present to the senses and what seems most remote has implications for the fictional presentation of setting, incident and character, and most especially for the relationship between author, narrator and reader. Many of Hardy's stories claim an origin in local traditions, and articulate their relationship to those origins and to the destination of a present-day readership in the layering of narrative and the invocation of prior authorities, sometimes a variety of different sources. The production of sophisticated written texts on the basis of remembered anecdotes raises far-reaching questions about the cultural status of literary work that proposes itself as the last in a series of successive versions, the one that gives definition and finish to the oral convention of improvisation. In *Wessex Tales*, Hardy published the earliest instances of something he returns to periodically in the short-story genre, revealing his fascination with the Napoleonic wars as a phase of British history still within living memory but culturally very distant from the late nineteenth-century outlook; a time of national crisis that brought international concerns into remote and isolated pockets of traditional life in the place he called Wessex. It was an important setting for his exploration of the constantly changing interrelations of traditional and modern, native and foreign, ideas and practices, and for the strong vein of thought and feeling in his work that cannot resist speculation about how things might have been different, how lives might have been lived differently. Some of the most interesting of Hardy's plots actually enclose these alternatives within the scope of lives that appear to return to normal after the 'interlude' in which the possibilities take shape. The sense of loss and gain, the delicate negotiation between acceptance and suppression, arising from the investigation of interludes is part of what gives these stories their power and strangeness.

Chapter 2 focuses on *A Group of Noble Dames*. Hardy placed this book under the heading of 'romances and fantasies', and this may have been a strategy, conscious or not, to distance himself from their sensational impact and the criticism he would receive from a worried editor of the *Graphic*, in which periodical the stories were to be serialised. Hardy may have considered them romances and fantasies, but they were purported to be based upon county records and histories of local 'Wessex' families, and they alarmed the *Graphic* editor accordingly with their subject-matter of illegitimacy, adultery, secret marriages and non-marriages. Hardy's problems with censorship and 'Grundyism' in this case were a preamble to the shocked reception his next serial for the *Graphic* would receive: *Tess of the d'Urbervilles* was serialised later in the same year. *A Group of Noble Dames* offers fascinating insights into Hardy's near-obsession in his mature phase with the marriage contract, and with its legal and immutable binding of erratic and mutable men and women. Its prevalent themes are of class difference, ancestry and mental torture; and it contains striking examples of experimental ideas about sexual politics, including an effective reversal of the stereotypical male gaze. It explores further the nature of the relationship between subjectivity and historical time, often approached through a tension between precipitancy and belatedness, and it introduces a major theme of the final phase of Hardy's fiction in its scrutiny of the mistreatment of children.

In *Life's Little Ironies*, the subject of Chapter 3, the fate of children is not only an issue in its own right, but is related to the question of cultural legacy and of writing as testimony to a past whose experience must be transmitted to the future. In this respect, *Life's Little Ironies* is the most volatile of Hardy's volumes of short fiction, in its constant remodelling of narrative point of view and in its antagonistic relationship with the reader. At a time when Hardy's attitude towards the audience for his novels was becoming increasingly disillusioned and mistrustful, these often disturbing and provocative stories no longer court their readers but challenge them, with a succession of moods and tactics of dogmatism, satire, sentiment and sometimes bleak indifference. Thematically central to this uneasy stand-off with an unreliable readership is the story 'On the Western Circuit', which revolves around the fatal ramifications of misreading. Hardy works towards a concept of social identity as coded performance that depends on the readability of a limited range of options. The misconstructions of the three characters at the centre of the story arise from their desires and ambitions exceeding the containment strategies of available discourses and institutions. The poetics of the short story is at its most complex and unpredictable in these texts.

Chapter 4 analyses the most uneven of Hardy's volumes of short stories, *A Changed Man*, published thirteen years after the composition in 1900 of his last statement of prose narrative, the story of the same name. Distortions, discrepancies and discontinuities form the subject-matter of these tales. Distortions of the seen and heard, discrepancies between word and deed, and especially between the performative language of the marriage contract and its actual consequences, in discontinuous lives, are the themes of these stories which powerfully reiterate major concerns across Hardy's work of misapprehension, mischance and misalliance. These tales are the exception to the chronologically concentrated groups of stories previously published, although they include a core of six texts all written in the 1890s and 1900. These return to the Napoleonic scenario, using the figure of the soldier to counterpoint inward-looking and outward-looking attitudes and customs, and they are concerned above all with failed connections between individuals and communities. In the 1897 story, 'The Grave by the Handpost', as in *Tess of the d'Urbervilles*, a letter is accidentally swept away with cruelly ironic consequences, as a man's final wishes concerning his burial, declared in the letter, are left unheeded. Hardy died fifteen years after the final publication of this story in *A Changed Man*, and his own wishes over his burial were left unheeded. Those closest to him thought Hardy's burial in Westminster Abbey one of 'life's little ironies', bearing witness to the distortions and refractions of his life in his art.

All references to Hardy's short stories are to the Library Edition published by Macmillan.

Acknowledgements

I would like to thank J. Hillis Miller for his support and encouragement over the years, especially because it was in his class on the short story at Yale that I first studied some of the tales discussed in this volume; these pages are indebted to his work on Hardy. I would also like to thank Gillian Beer for her continuing help and guidance ever since my first approach to Hardy's fiction, while writing my book *Ancestry and Narrative*. I am also very grateful for the support and understanding of Robert Hampson, my Head of Department at Royal Holloway.

Sophie Gilmartin

I would like to thank my colleague, Leo Mellor, for many insights while sharing the enjoyable burden of teaching a course on the short story.

Rod Mengham

We both wish to acknowledge Martin Ray's indispensable research on the textual history of the short stories. Our two readers for Edinburgh University Press made many helpful and insightful suggestions, and we thank them for the thoughtfulness that they brought to this task. We would like to thank Jackie Jones of Edinburgh University Press, for the kindness, encouragement and patience she showed during the preparation of the manuscript. We have also appreciated the care and efficiency of the production team.

Textual Note

Except where otherwise indicated, page references to Hardy's novels, short stories and prefaces are given in parentheses within the text, and are taken from the Macmillan Library Edition of Hardy's works, published at various dates between 1949 and 1952. This edition, based on the Macmillan Wessex edition of 1912–13, also includes Hardy's revisions of 1919, and is widely available and authoritative. It includes all four volumes of the short stories. Please see the bibliography for more details of the specific volumes of the Library Edition referred to in this book. References to the volumes of short stories are indicated by page number in parentheses unless the volume is unclear from the context. References to the novels will be indicated by an abbreviation of the title and the page number.

There are two excellent recent editions of *Wessex Tales* and *Life's Little Ironies*, edited for Oxford University Press by Kathryn R. King and Alan Manford respectively. For the sake of uniformity we did not use these editions for page references, but further details of these OUP editions are given in the bibliography. Pamela Dalziel has edited stories which were uncollected by Hardy in his lifetime, also for Oxford University Press, entitled *An Indiscretion in the Life of an Heiress and other Stories*. While these stories do not fall within the scope of this study, which concentrates on those works Hardy wished to collect into the four volumes of his short fiction, we do discuss some of these tales and our references are then to Pamela Dalziel's excellent edition.

Also included within parentheses in the text are page references to Michael Millgate's edition of *The Life and Work of Thomas Hardy* (Macmillan, 1984), abbreviated as *Life*.

Chapter 1

Wessex Tales

Thomas Hardy's peculiar, idiosyncratic vision can move from a sweeping view of a vast landscape to fix upon the insects which occupy its smallest spaces; it is this eye that has led many to describe his writing as cinematic. Indeed David Lodge has written that Hardy's 'verbal description [. . .] can be readily analysed in cinematic terms: long shot, close-up, wide angle, telephoto, zoom, etc'.[1] But rather than the camera lens it was in fact the telescope, 'the big brass telescope that had been handed on in the family', that was instrumental in developing his way of seeing from boyhood.[2] Throughout Hardy's childhood, the Sunday walk would take his family together southwards along the heath to a 'silent green pond' called Rushy-Pond, and from there they would ascend to a high point topped by a tumulus known as Rainbarrow. Hardy's friend in later life, the Dorset photographer Hermann Lea, recounts how from Rainbarrow, 'with the aid of a telescope, his father would point out places of interest, houses and other buildings on which he was then working.'[3] Between 1914 and 1916, before the First World War made petrol scarce, Lea drove Hardy 'many thousands of miles in my motor car'. Their destinations, mapped out by Hardy upon the ordnance survey maps that he loved, were often high places: 'he always wanted to reach high points: "and please don't forget to bring your glasses", he used to say to me when we set out for some high point, my binoculars having superseded the old telescope'.[4] From his early years to late in life, Hardy saw his environment in ways akin to a telescopic sweeping view of the landscape which can then focus in to an intimate concentration upon objects as minute as the veins in a rabbit's ear, such as the almost blindly myopic Clym Yeobright can make out in *The Return of the Native*. Hardy's imaginatively posthumous poem, 'Afterwards', acknowledges his peculiar range of vision which can notice both 'when the hedgehog travels furtively over the lawn' and 'the full-starred heavens that winter sees': great and small, 'He was a man who used to notice such things'.[5]

Another important moment with the telescope occurred one morning in July 1856 when Hardy was sixteen. Remembering before breakfast that there was to be a hanging at Dorchester gaol, he took up the family telescope and made the solitary journey over the heath again to the high slope by Rushy-Pond. As he recounts in the *Life*:

> The sun behind his back shone straight on the white stone façade of the gaol, the gallows upon it, and the form of the murderer in white fustian, the executioner and officials in dark clothing, and the crowd below, being invisible at this distance of three miles. At the moment of his placing the glass to his eye the white figure dropped downwards, and the faint note of the town clock struck eight.
>
> The whole thing had been so sudden that the glass nearly fell from Hardy's hands. He seemed alone on the heath with the hanged man; and he crept homeward wishing he had not been so curious. (*Life*, 33)

Hardy uses aspects of this experience in his story 'The Withered Arm' from *Wessex Tales*. Gertrude Lodge rides across Egdon Heath to find a ghastly cure for her blighted arm at the Casterbridge assizes. She pauses at 'a pool called Rushy-Pond', and, as Hardy and his father had done, surveys the landscape, finding a point upon it which marks her personal interest:

> Over the railing she saw the low green country; over the green trees the roofs of the town; over the roofs a white flat façade, denoting the entrance to the county jail. On the roof of this front specks were moving about; they seemed to be workmen erecting something. Her flesh crept. (99)

Gertrude does not view this through a telescope, but the language here describes a gradual focusing from general landscape to the particular and personal; from Rushy-Pond (personal to Hardy) to the spot in the distance which holds an especial interest for Gertrude, then back to focus upon the woman's skin, and the gooseflesh rising upon it in a visceral response to what she has seen upon the landscape stretching before her. Her chilled reaction to the sudden focus upon the gallows relives Hardy's shock at the sight of the condemned man dropping to his death. For Hardy and for Gertrude Lodge, everything else in the landscape is, as Hardy wrote in the *Life*, suddenly 'invisible': all else falls away and they feel alone with the hanged man, or his means of death in the form of the gallows. The sharp focusing which can render all else invisible is linked to Hardy's very particular mapping of the landscape which is seen very distinctly in *Wessex Tales*. His gaze sweeps easily over an environment unimpeded by boundaries, objects, actions or people unnecessary to his 'moments of vision' (the title of his 1917 volume of poetry), or to his narrative: they become 'invisible' as did the officials and the crowd at the Dorchester hanging that he witnessed through the telescope. Of course this particularity in viewing the environment is common to most narrative description, which cannot describe everything but must decide and highlight what will be brought forward for the reader's notice. But Hardy foregrounds this particularity, producing what Ralph Pite has described as 'a blank, extensive environment'.[6] Upon this blankness he maps marks as ephemeral as a hedgehog's tracks, human footprints in the dew, or as long-standing and obdurate as Stonehenge. The telescope serves both practically and figuratively to emphasise how Hardy's focus on his object is so intense as to leave all else momentarily invisible; but his point of view-taking is, like the height by Rushy-Pond, a place of personal relevance, not far from home.

Wessex Tales, comprising the stories that Hardy gathered together to be published in 1888,[7] is the only volume of fiction in his *oeuvre* to be named for that invented region, his single most famous creation of place, which even in his own time so entered the cultural imagination that Hardy acknowledged that his 'dream-country has, by degrees, solidified into a utilitarian region which people can go to, take a house in, and write to the papers from'.[8] However, Hardy's telescopic gaze could move freely over the landscape of his 'dream-country'; imaginatively and physically, 'Wessex' was an environment across which the uncluttered spaces offered a freedom of movement. Most of the stories in this volume are set in a period at least thirty-five years before their telling. The Wessex landscape reflects this, as can be seen in Hardy's description of Gertrude's movement across Egdon Heath in 'The Withered Arm':

> Enclosure Acts had not taken effect, and the banks and fences which now exclude the cattle of those villagers who formerly enjoyed rights of commonage thereon, and the carts of those who had turbary privileges which kept them in firing all the year round, were not erected. Gertrude, therefore, rode along with no other obstacles than the prickly furze bushes, the mats of heather, the white water courses, and the natural steeps and declivities of the ground. (99)

Gertrude moves through a landscape unimpeded by 'banks and fences' placed there later by a central government's Act, and Hardy himself described in his autobiography how he was able to move both imaginatively and literally through 'Wessex', unfettered and unmindful of the legal divisions of county boundaries: in his writings, he,

> obliterates the names of the six counties whose area he traverses in his scenes under the general appellation of 'Wessex' – an old word that became quite popular after the date of *Far From The Madding Crowd*, where he first introduced it. So far did he carry this idea of the unity of Wessex that he used to say he had grown to forget the crossing of county boundaries within the ancient Kingdom . . . . (*Life*, 126)

To return to Egdon Heath, Ralph Pite's consideration of Hardy's maps of Wessex compares them to the Egdon envisioned in the opening chapters of *The Return of the Native*. As in the movement of both the fictional Gertrude Lodge and Hardy, the landscape offers an imaginatively open space which obliterates more recent legal boundaries, and recognises the local marks made by ancient and modern men and women. Pite describes the map:

> A blank, extensive environment is given, then 'humanity appears', on a road and moving between points on the ground. There is an elemental, unmarked quality to the land which draws attention to the human movements which cross it, marking on its surface roads, paths and railway lines.[9]

The importance of the human figure, the human mark or impression on the landscape is borne out almost obsessively in Hardy's works. In the *Life*, he includes a journal entry for 28 September 1877:

> An object or mark raised or made by man on a scene is worth ten times any such formed by unconscious Nature. Hence clouds, mists, and mountains are unimportant beside the wear on a threshold, or the print of a hand. (*Life*, 120)

And thirty-five years later his poem 'At Castle Boterel' recalls a single moment when he and his wife Emma climbed a steep road together in their early courtship. The fifth stanza makes a daring assertion:

> Primaeval rocks form the road's steep border,
> And much have they faced there, first and last,
> Of the transitory in Earth's long order;
> But what they record in colour and cast
> Is – that we two passed.[10]

The most important time that the geological record marks here is a human moment in which two lovers passed by, engaged in an inconsequential and now forgotten conversation. The hill road that they walked becomes a feature of Hardy's highly subjective inner mapping of Wessex, although it does not appear on the Wessex maps that Hardy authorised for the collected edition of 1895–6, and later the 1912–13 edition of his works. The reason it does not appear is of course partly a matter of scale. Ralph Pite notices that the maps of Wessex that accompany Hardy's editions are 'uncluttered' and relatively 'unmarked' because they refer mainly to places that appear in his writing.[11] But if Hardy were to trace onto a physical map the narrative mapping and marking of Wessex that he produces in the novels, poetry and short stories, the map would have to be on an impossibly enlarged scale: it would need to include 'the wear on a threshold, or the print of a hand'. Indeed, 'the print of a hand' is at the centre of the fourth story of *Wessex Tales*, 'The Withered Arm', in which the spurned Rhoda Brook 'overlooks' her rival, causing the imprint of her grasping hand to appear on Gertrude's arm, shrivelling and disabling it. This would seem to confuse geographical landscape with the landscape of the body, the map with skin, but this is precisely what Hardy does again and again, and this relationship between marking on the body and on the landscape is prevalent in *Wessex Tales*.

Marking and impression preoccupied Hardy as he made some of his early notes for the short stories that would come to make up *Wessex Tales*. On a single page of journal entries reproduced in the *The Life*, three of the six entries concern marking on the body, the character or the landscape. One from 28 September 1877 is quoted above, and the two that precede it, also for 1877, are as follows:

> July 13. The sudden disappointment of a hope leaves a scar which the ultimate fulfilment of that hope never entirely removes.
>
> July 27. James Bushrod of Broadmayne saw the two German soldiers [of the York Hussars] shot [for desertion] on Bincombe Down in 1801. It was in the path across the down, or near it. James Selby of the same village thinks there is a mark. [The tragedy was used in 'The Melancholy Hussar', the real names of the deserters being given]. (*Life*, 119)

The 13 July entry is especially appropriate to the fifth story of the collection, 'Fellow-Townsmen' (1880). In this story, the character Barnet reads two letters separated by an interval of a few minutes; the first announces the death of his estranged wife, leaving him free to marry his first love, and the second invites him to the wedding of that first love to his closest friend:

> That his few minutes of hope, between the reading of the first and second letters, had carried him to extraordinary heights of rapture was proved by the immensity of his suffering now. The sun blazing into his face would have shown a close watcher that a horizontal line, which had never been seen before, but which was never to be gone thereafter, was somehow gradually forming itself in the smooth of his forehead. (157)

Hardy grouped *Wessex Tales* with his 'Novels of Character and Environment', so the marking upon landscape, body and character (or how the scarring of the psyche appears physically on the body) is highly appropriate to the concerns of this category. A brief consideration of another novel which Hardy included among those of 'character and environment' – *Tess of the d'Urbervilles* – will serve to introduce and to highlight how disappointment, labour, injustice and fear produced by the environment are translated onto the body and character in *Wessex Tales*.

In his seminal analysis of repetition in *Tess of the d'Urbervilles*, J. Hillis Miller draws attention to the marking of Tess's body by sexual violation as belonging to 'a chain of figures of speech in the novel, a chain that includes the tracing of a pattern, the making of a mark, the carving of a line or sign, and the act of writing.'[12] He begins his analysis with the famous lacuna that ends 'Phase the First' of the novel in which the narrator asks why it was that Tess should have been violated: 'Why it was that upon this beautiful feminine tissue, sensitive as gossamer, and practically blank as snow as yet, there should have been traced such a coarse pattern as it was doomed to receive' (*Tess*, 91). Miller argues that,

> The metaphor of the tracing of a pattern has a multiple significance. It assimilates the real event to the act of writing about it. It defines both the novel and the events it represents as repetitions, as the outlining again of a pattern which already somewhere exists. Tess's violation exists, both when it 'first' happens and in the narrator's telling, as the re-enactment of an event which has already occurred. The physical act itself is the making of a mark, the outlining of a sign. This deprives the event of any purely present existence and makes it a design referring backward and forward to a long chain of similar events throughout history.[13]

To regard Tess's violation as an event in 'a long chain of similar events throughout history' could be seen as somewhat reminiscent of the fatalistic acceptance by 'Tess's own people down in those retreats' who 'never tired of saying [. . .]: "It was to be"' (*Tess*, 91): it has happened before, it will happen again, it will always be 'on the cards'. But Hardy struggles with this repetition; his writing seems poised between an acknowledgement that repetition is inescapable, that social and sexual injustice will happen again, and, on the other hand, that it should not happen again, that possibly his exposure of these injustices may help to allay the possibility of their repetition, even as he ironically retraces and repeats their occurrence, as Miller writes, in his own narratives.

The only 'reason' given, to be almost immediately dismissed, as to 'why [. . .] there should have been traced such a coarse pattern' upon Tess's skin, 'practically blank as snow' – is 'the possibility of retribution. Doubtless some of Tess d'Urberville's armoured ancestors rollicking home from a fray had dealt the same measure even more ruthlessly towards peasant girls of their time.' Here we move from Tess's skin, which was unmarked, but has now been 'traced' with a coarse pattern, to her ancestral landscape, across which move her ruthless ancestors, setting their violating mark upon peasant girls like Tess. She oddly becomes both victim and perpetrator in this moment: by her sex and class she is victim, but genetically, genealogically, she is a violator, and we see another brief moment of this when she later strikes Alec d'Urberville with her 'gauntlet', as her armoured ancestors may have done, causing him to bleed. Of course Tess Durbeyfield is a victim – she is not responsible for 'the sins of the fathers'. But Hardy's brief suggestion that her violation was retribution, and his juxtaposition of the untraced landscape of her body and the 'rollicking' of her ancestors across the Wessex landscape, further demonstrates how he is preoccupied with the marking of body and land, and also how the injustices of poverty, oppression and neglect, for example, may finally rebound upon the perpetrators, as well as oppressing the victim. These injustices, once set in place, may inhere in the environment for many generations. This will be crucial to a consideration of Hardy's great short story, 'The Withered Arm'.

Tess's body is marked by labour where the stubble of the hayfield makes her arm bleed, by sexual violation, and by sexual oppression when she 'mutilates' herself, cutting off her eyebrows to deflect unwelcome attention, and finally by the mark of the hangman's rope. This last mark we do not see directly, but in two stories of *Wessex Tales* that mark is directly spoken of or seen. Both 'The Withered Arm' and 'The Three Strangers' are set in the late 1820s or the 1830s, a period of great agricultural depression in Britain, especially affecting south-western England. 'The Three Strangers' is dated more specifically than any of the stories in *Wessex Tales*: all the action takes place on the night of 28 March 182-, and even though the events of the tale have taken place 'fifty years' before its narration, the date can presumably be remembered so exactly because it marks the occasion of the christening party for Shepherd Fennel's second daughter. On this night of torrential rain, 'nineteen persons' are gathered in the Fennel's cottage in a remote and exposed part of the down to sing, dance and drink the Fennels' mead, celebrating a ritual of family and community life. But the evening also marks another ritual: it is the last night alive for Timothy Summers, a starving clock-maker who stole a sheep in broad daylight to feed his family. He is to be hanged the next morning at eight o'clock, but has escaped to arrive at Shepherd Fennel's house as the first 'stranger' of the tale. In another story from *Wessex Tales*, 'Interlopers at the Knap', Farmer Darton comments on his own fate as he travels to meet his betrothed; 'Ay – call it my fate! Hanging and wiving go by destiny' (179). But, while the farmer facetiously juxtaposes these two rituals, as if they are both part of a 'natural' set of circumstances, inevitable and pre-determined, the revellers at Shepherd Fennel's reveal themselves over the course of the story as resistant to the rituals of the hangman. In the midst of celebrating one of their religious and communal rituals of life, they reject with horror the ritual of death which is arrogantly and bluntly celebrated by 'the man in cinder-grey' – the hangman who has sheltered from the rain and joined their party.

Public hangings, or the 'hang-fair' as it is called in 'The Withered Arm', were extremely popular events in the nineteenth century, attracting huge crowds to the county towns. In 1868 public hangings were abolished and performed behind prison walls, but Hardy in his youth witnessed two, the first, as he writes in *The Life*, of a woman 'when he stood close to the gallows' (33). He writes in the Preface to *Wessex Tales* that 'in the neighbourhood of county-towns hanging matters used to form a large proportion of the local tradition' (v). Hardy grew up fascinated and deeply affected by these local traditions, and the stories of hanging related by his parents. The impression that these scenes of execution made upon the young Hardy is retraced in 'The Withered Arm' and 'The Three Strangers'. In the latter story, the focus is especially upon the personality and celebrity of the hangman. Hardy's account of conversations as a boy with the man who failed to get the job of chief executioner, told in the Preface to *Wessex Tales*, may shed some light on the disturbing presence of the second stranger to enter Shepherd Fennel's cottage.

In the Preface, Hardy writes that he had in boyhood,

> the privilege of being on speaking terms with a man who applied for the office [of chief executioner], and who sank into an incurable melancholy because he failed to get it, some slight mitigation of his grief being to dwell upon striking episodes in the lives of those happier ones who had held it with success and renown. (v)

But to the young Hardy and to his ambitious and disappointed acquaintance, 'the nobleness [of the profession] was never questioned' (vi).

The office of executioner always attracted numerous applicants for the job in the nineteenth century, even though it was not especially well-paid. One has to infer that the theatricality, the power and the ritualistic nature of the execution held a fascination for those who wanted the position. A man did not have to be educated to become a hangman – after all, the hangman in 'The Withered Arm' is also a 'jobbing gardener' – but his job gave him the right to stand beside the sheriff, chaplain and surgeon on a stage before thousands. There, after prayers and a special order of words and ceremony, the hangman would be the centre of attention, aside from the person to be hanged. Such was the macabre prestige of the position that Hardy as a boy wondered why his acquaintance, 'could not have aimed at something more commonplace – that would have afforded him more chances – such as the office of a judge, a bishop, or even a Member of Parliament' (v–vi). The 'nobleness' of the hangman's office raised him above some of the highest legal, religious and political officers in Hardy's youthful imagination. However, the high repute of the profession and what it represents are certainly called into question in the person of the hangman in 'The Three Strangers'.

Although the fact is not declared until close to the end of the story, the first stranger to seek shelter in the lonely cottage is Timothy Summers, just escaped from the county jail in a desperate bid to escape his hanging the next morning. When the second stranger enters, he joins Summers in the chimney corner and proceeds to enjoy himself, drinking far more of the Fennel's best mead than the frugal wife wishes to part with. He calls rudely for more, as if at an inn rather than relying upon the generosity of strangers, and the ruffled Mrs Fennel whispers to her husband, that the man is 'a stranger unbeknown to any of us. For my part, I don't like the look of the man at all' (15). Her unease about this stranger is gradually felt by all in the cottage, as the stranger who had been playfully coy when asked about the nature of his work, begins to drop hints about his trade. The hedge-carpenter observes, 'You may generally tell what a man is by his claws [. . .]. My fingers be as full of thorns as an old pin-cushion is of pins'. The second stranger responds 'smartly': 'True; but the oddity of my trade is that instead of setting a mark upon me, it sets a mark upon my customers'. He then breaks into a three-verse song, in which he is joined solely by Timothy Summers who desperately feigns ease and joviality to disguise his position as the stranger's next 'customer'. The song spells out to his audience that he is the hangman: 'For my customers I tie, and take them upon high, And waft 'em to a far countree' (16–17). The effect upon those gathered for the christening is as if a devil had come into their midst and they form a 'remote circle' around him.

Removed from the context of the gallows, the hangman is no longer dignified or noble, but a sleek, self-satisfied 'King's man'. Indifferent, and even jovial, about the life he is to take the next morning, he keeps his hands clean; he is left unmarked by his profession, and simply regards it as a job by which others are 'marked' by him. The hangman, who has come from another county town to perform the job, is doubly alien to the cottagers when dissociated from the context of the 'hang-fair'. Seeing the hangman in their own domestic and communal circle, removed from the theatrical, solemn context of the gallows, brings revelation to the cottagers: this man may represent the 'King's justice', but with his greed, arrogance and disrespect for the local man who is to die, he also represents a fearful injustice which they begin to voice among themselves and to question:

> 'He's come to do it! 'Tis to be at Casterbridge jail to-morrow – the man for sheep-stealing – the poor clock-maker we heard of, who used to live away at Shottsford and had no work to do – Timothy Summers, whose family were a-starving, and so he went out of Shottsford by the high-road, and took a sheep in open daylight, defying the farmer and the farmer's wife and the farmer's lad, and every man jack among 'em'. (18)

In this passage, sympathy for the starving man evolves into admiration for a folk-hero, and as the time of the story's setting is one of severe agricultural depression, of the Tolpuddle martyrs and Chartism, their language could adumbrate the political awakening and resistance of the nineteen friends gathered at Shepherd Fennel's. This is not quite borne out by the ensuing events however. A third stranger enters, stares in terror at the hangman as he sings a final verse of his executioner's song, and disappears into the night. Shortly after, a distant gun is heard firing from the county town, announcing that a prisoner has escaped. The hangman uses his authority as a King's justice to send the men out after the third stranger whom they all believe to be the escaped prisoner, and they all go. Only after they have returned with the quiet third stranger does this man reveal that his suspicious behaviour arose from his horror upon entering the cottage, at seeing the hangman singing in the chimney corner with his brother, the prisoner who is to be hanged. The resistance to the King's justice after this is passive but effective. Ordered by the authorities over the ensuing days to find the fugitive, they appear to comply, searching, but making sure they never find Timothy Summers. Just as they had closed ranks, forming a 'remote circle' around the hangman, so they resist central authority by championing the local man whose name they knew, and decide a better justice for him.

It has often been said that Hardy was cautious, indeed cagey, about expressing his political views. In the *Life* however, he described himself as a young man 'with a passion for reforming the world', holding 'socialistic, not to say revolutionary' beliefs which received expansive treatment in his first unpublished novel, *The Poor Man and the Lady* (*Life*, 63). That novel being destroyed, we cannot turn to it for his more directly stated political views, but in fact his notebooks and journals often reveal a sharp and at times corrosive handling of the social and political scene. One such journal entry, written after attending a dinner in Camden in July 1891 expresses some of the contempt for the political and legal authority of the centre:

> the talk was entirely political – of when the next election would be – of the probable Prime Minister – of ins and outs – of Lord This and the Duke of That – everything except the people for whose existence alone these politicians exist. Their welfare is never once thought of. (*Life*, 249)

Admittedly the potential radicalism of his criticism here is mitigated by the fact that it is given within a private journal, that he only allowed to be published after his death. The narrator of 'The Three Strangers' eschews any such direct statements of social or political views. In fact, the narratorial stance is elusive – distanced and yet present. The narrator is not omniscient; in describing the location of Shepherd Fennel's cottage he tells that, 'Fifty years ago such a lonely cottage stood on such a down, and may possibly be standing there now' (3). The events and conversation inside the cottage are given as if the narrator were either omniscient or present, but at no point does the narrator declare his presence. He remains a step apart, but is not a fourth stranger.

The narrator opens the tale by explaining and translating to an urban readership the nature and names of the 'furzy downs, coombs, or ewe-leases, as they are called according to their kind, that fill a large area of certain counties in the south and south-west'. This area has 'an appearance but little modified by the lapse of centuries. If any mark of human occupation is met with hereon, it usually takes the form of the solitary cottage of some shepherd' (3). Again, Hardy moves from the vast landscape and timeframe in this story to the particular: Shepherd Fennel's cottage is that 'mark of human occupation' on the landscape, and one night at a christening party in that place is set against 'the lapse of centuries' (3). In fact it is not just a single night, but a single moment of recognition between brothers which sets them apart as 'marked men': when Timothy Summers' brother recognises him and the hangman together in the cottage, the moment of terror seems to ingrain his sadness and trouble over his brother's fate upon his body. Although he is released from suspicion, 'he looked nothing the less sad on that account, it being beyond the power of magistrate or constable to raze out the written troubles in his brain, for they concerned another whom he regarded with more solicitude than himself' (28). Like the 'coarse pattern' that was traced upon Tess d'Urberville's flesh, the mind of Summers' unnamed brother has been written upon by sorrow and injustice. The narrator's ironic political commentary comes through here, as of course it is the legal system represented by the constable, magistrate and the hangman that have marked the fugitive's brother, and declared the fugitive as a 'marked man' for all his days. The particularly callous hangman of 'The Three Strangers' enjoys the fact that it is the nature of his 'trade' to remain unmarked by his labours (he is unimpressed by the sorrows of his 'customers'), but to leave a mark on others. The fact that Timothy Summers escapes the physical mark of the hangman's rope is cause for celebration among the sympathetic country people of the area, as it is also for the present but distanced narrator who takes a step forward and closer at the end of the story to declare directly that 'the intended punishment was cruelly disproportionate to the transgression' (28).

The hangman's mark, 'a line the colour of an unripe blackberry', which surrounds a hanged boy's neck in 'The Withered Arm', is just one of the many marks which mar the lives of this story's characters. They represent impressions upon the body of poverty and labour, and of injustices which cross class and gender lines. The initial focus of 'The Withered Arm' is on the character of Rhoda Brook, a thirty-year-old milkmaid, whose son is the illegitimate child of one Farmer Lodge. The story opens with Rhoda hearing about the imminent marriage of Lodge to a pretty, younger woman. Understandably jealous, Rhoda dreams of fighting with the young woman, named Gertrude, who appears in the dream as a threatening incubus whom Rhoda only just manages to fend off: she 'seized the confronting spectre by its obtrusive left arm, and whirled it backward to the floor' (77–8). At the same time, while Gertrude is sound asleep, 'dreaming I was away in some strange place, a pain suddenly shot into my arm there, and was so keen as to awaken me' (80). From this point on, her arm starts to wither. The two women subsequently become friends, and Gertrude persuades Rhoda to lead her to an exorcist, Conjuror Trendle, in the hope of discovering a cure for her steadily worsening affliction. This first visit is inconclusive, except that Gertrude has the face of her enemy revealed to her, and it is fairly obvious that this is Rhoda's face. Her arm becomes so disfigured that her husband finds her repellent, and in her desperation, Gertrude returns to Conjuror Trendle on her own, only to be told that the only solution to her problem is to touch with the withered limb the neck of a man who has just been hanged. Gertrude waits and waits for a hanging, and when one is finally announced, manages to persuade the hangman to give her access to the corpse. At the very moment she touches the neck of the corpse with her arm, a shriek causes her to turn round and discover that among those present are Rhoda Brook and her own husband, making it clear in an instant that the dead malefactor is their son. The shock kills Gertrude.

This is among the most sensational stories that Hardy ever wrote, well-suited to the preferences of the readers of *Blackwood's Edinburgh Magazine*, where it first appeared in 1888, two years after the publication of *The Mayor of Casterbridge*. But although the story has a fairy-tale structure, suggesting how easily it might be detached from this particular time and place, it is in fact impossible to extricate it from its Victorian ideological setting. From the beginning, the reader's attention is drawn to the impoverished circumstances of Rhoda and her son. Rhoda's own thinness and gauntness are reproduced in the state of her cottage, which is built of simple mud walls, 'while here and there in the thatch above a rafter showed like a bone protruding through the skin' (71). It is a small building with no back door, and is surrounded by 'leaner pastures' (74). Rhoda is evidently embittered and her son also has a 'somewhat hard nature' (75); their difficult lives and physical constraint are contrasted with the sleekness and complacency of Farmer Lodge, whose complete lack of integrity is suggested in his appearance when he drives home his new young wife, 'cleanly shaven like an actor, his face being toned to that bluish-vermilion hue which so often graces a thriving farmer's features when returning home after successful dealings in the town' (72).

A very simple and obvious counterpoint is set up between the farmer and the family he will not own up to, between their mud cottage and his 'white house of ample dimensions' (73). This is unremarkable. What is remarkable is that the power Rhoda is supposed to be able to exert over Gertrude depends on the milkmaid being able to 'raise a mental image of the unconscious Mrs Lodge that was realistic as a photograph' (76). And what is extraordinary is that Rhoda forms this image without ever having clapped eyes on Gertrude herself. All she has to go on is the description of Gertrude given to her by her son, and this is crucial because it indicates that the story's interest is concentrated in images of people that can be detached from their actual personalities. Rhoda apparently does her damage to Gertrude knowing only an image that is not even that of the real Gertrude. Rhoda's jealousy and Gertrude's anxiety about her arm are what rule their lives, in a world in which, as Gertrude says, 'men think so much of personal appearance' (83). Rhoda's obsessive questions to her son, who has seen Gertrude before she has, are all concerned with her rival's physical appearance; her hair colour, her height, her hands, and whether she 'shows marks of the lady on her, as I expect she do' (71). The 'blasting' of Gertrude's arm, although it seems so fantastic, is actually a means of gauging the sheer force of women's sexual anxieties. And when Rhoda finds out about it, she even begins to half-share the village people's superstition about her that she has the powers of a witch: 'O, can it be,' she said to herself, when her visitor had departed, 'that I exercise a malignant power over people against my own will?' (81).

The truth is that she is the agent of a malignant power; the story makes this power an occult one, but its real sphere of operation is an ideological one, the 'ideology of femininity' identified by George Wotton[14] and Penny Boumelha,[15] according to which women think of themselves primarily in terms of how they are seen by men. As far as Rhoda herself is aware, 'something in her own individuality seemed to convict [her] of crime' (82). She is not the source of evil, but is made to suspect that she is because of the feelings of guilt that issue inevitably from the conditions of sexual rivalry which determine the relations of women under the gaze of men: 'In her secret heart Rhoda did not altogether object to a slight diminution of her successor's beauty' (83). The bitter irony that enters into the situation of these two particular women is that they develop a touching closeness to one other. Rhoda comes to be seized by dread lest 'her character in the eyes of the most useful friend she had ever had be ruined irretrievably' (86). The epithet 'useful' makes her attitude sound a manipulative one, but their mutual expectations of one another are not as selfish as that makes it sound. They are rivals who nevertheless understand and sympathise with one another's problems. They are capable of an unusual closeness but are held back by an awareness of their social function in the eyes of men, which puts them into cruel opposition. As Gertrude's condition deteriorates, a rumour goes round that the 'gradual loss of the use of her left arm was owing to her being "overlooked" by Rhoda Brook' (90). This term, 'overlooking', seems to be capable of a very wide application in a society where 'men think so much of personal appearance'. If the country people intend it to mean that Gertrude has been hexed in some way by Rhoda Brook, there is another sense in which the gaze of men in general hexes the lives of women in general. The more Farmer Lodge becomes disgusted by his wife's disfigurement, the more she becomes obsessed with that image of herself from which she has been parted, so that 'her closet was lined with bottled, packets and ointment-pots of every description' (91). She is 'craving for renewed love, through the medium of renewed beauty' (95). From one point of view, the outlandishness of the cure prescribed to her is no more outlandish, no more outrageous or unreasonable, than the complaint she is suffering from, and that consists of the expectations that men have for the lives of women. The ultimately demoralising effect of this ideological pressure is seen in the bizarre prayers that Gertrude offers each night: 'O Lord, hang some guilty or innocent person soon!' (96).

In the early novels *Under the Greenwood Tree* (1872) and *Far from the Madding Crowd* (1874), there is a persistent emphasis on both 'overlooking' and 'picturing'; these activities are related to one another and geared to the idea of control over the object of the gaze. There is a particularly striking instance of this kind of correlation in the description of an episode from Hardy's own life, on the occasion when he witnessed the public execution of a woman and clearly derived some form of sexual excitement from doing so.[16] 'The Withered Arm' is a story concerned with 'overlooking' and sexual rivalry, culminating in a public execution that, quite apart from Gertrude's special interest in it, is described first and foremost as a 'spectacle' as far as everyone else is concerned: 'some enthusiasts had been known to walk all the way to Casterbridge and back in one day, solely to witness the spectacle' (96). It was precisely this kind of enthusiasm, expressed in the same way, that Hardy had demonstrated himself. On 2 November 1904, as Robert Gittings relates, *The Sketch* printed a story told by Hardy to the journalist and novelist Neil Munro of the second hanging that Hardy had witnessed in his sixteenth year. The first, in July of 1856, Hardy saw through a telescope, as described in the beginning of this chapter. But the following month he walked to Dorchester to the 'hang-fair' with a friend, to see the execution of Martha Browne for the murder of her husband:

> Young Hardy, with another boy, came into Dorchester and witnessed the execution from a tree that overlooked the yard in which the gallows was placed. He never forgot the rustle of the thin black gown the woman was wearing as she was led forth by the warders. A penetrating rain was falling; the white cap was no sooner over the woman's head than it clung to her features, and the noose was put round the neck of what looked like a marble statue.[17]

In his biography of Hardy, Robert Gittings discusses this incident in Hardy's teenage life as one of sexual excitement, and draws attention to the fact that for Hardy, 'the rustle of a woman's dress had enormous sexual meaning'. As a child he harboured feelings 'almost like that of a lover' for the local lady of the manor, who was very fond of him. He loved 'the thrilling "frou-frou" of her four grey silk flounces when she had used to bend over him, and when they brushed against the font as she entered church on Sundays' (*Life*, 24, 104–5). Rhoda Brook's son is also taken with 'the youthful freshness' of Gertrude Lodge, his father's wife, and is extremely attentive to the rustle of her gown. He tells his mother that in church Gertrude's 'silver-coloured gownd [. . .] whewed and whistled so loud when it rubbed against the pews that the lady coloured up more than ever for very shame at the noise, and pulled it in to keep it from touching' (75). The condemned Martha Browne's gown excited Hardy with its rustle as she walked, but presumably the gown of the executed woman was also arousing as it would, like Gertrude's, have been 'pulled in' tight to her body: it was considered seemly for the executioner to tie a woman's gown close around her body with rope before she was hanged on high to discourage prurient interest from the crowd below, another indicator of the sexual interest in the hanging of a woman. But the gown would also have been 'pulled in' because the 'penetrating rain' which made the white cap cling to her features would also have made the 'thin black gown' cling to her body. It would seem that Gertrude, who is so concentrated upon regaining her sexual attractiveness to her husband, is also aroused by the fever of the hang-fair as she enters the town. She arrives in Casterbridge outside a harness maker's shop: ' "What is going on there?" she asked of the ostler. "Making the rope for tomorrow." She throbbed responsively, and contracted her arm' (100). 'Contracted' is a particularly unusual word to use in this context.

What is being presented in all these texts is an association of 'overlooking', a desire for control and indirect forms of sexual arousal. It is a moot point whether the ending of 'The Withered Arm' copes with the burden of this association, or whether it backs away from it in the final *frisson* of the plot development. The shock value of the ending does not obliterate entirely the reader's awareness that Hardy has introduced an element of the mundane into what would otherwise be an emphatically lurid scenario. The hangman turns out to be a rather timid and second-rate figure – a gardener and a bereaved parent – just as the conjuror, Trendle, had been a sensible, down-to-earth character who 'affected not to believe largely in his own powers' (88). He is immediately reminiscent of Fell, the weather prophet, in *The Mayor of Casterbridge*. But the appearance of the rather ordinary hangman towards the end of 'The Withered Arm' reminds us that the sensational elements of the story are primarily psychological rather than supernatural. The key point about the revelation of the criminal's identity at the end of the story is not so much that he is the son of Rhoda and Farmer Lodge as the question of how he came to be there.

The hangman tells the reader that the boy is being executed for arson, that he has 'only just turned eighteen, and only present by chance when the rick was fired. Howsomever, there's not much risk of it [of letting him off], as they are obliged to make an example of him, there having been so much destruction of property that way lately' (103). This disclosure ought to take the reader back to the beginning of the story, where there is plenty of evidence to show why the boy's being on the spot when the rick was fired would not have been 'by chance'. What little information we have about him includes the observation that 'he hated going afield on the farms' (78); he is apprehensive about leaving the house, about going on the errands his mother requires of him; he is disinclined. His 'somewhat hard nature' suggests that going outside might leave him vulnerable to something that has had the effect of hardening him. Going outside perhaps exposes him to jeering; he is likely to be victimised by other children because he is illegitimate. His mother's injunction, 'never to speak to anybody in that house [Lodge's farmhouse], or go near the place' (78), indicates the extent to which she and the boy segregate themselves from the rest of the community; they are outsiders. In a sense, the boy is doomed to be the scapegoat in this area, if anybody is. And when he is sent outside, it is usually on the kind of escapade that would lead to his arrest if he were caught: poaching. In the second section of the story, we hear his mother telling him, 'the hare you wired is very tender; but mind that nobody catches you' (75). In one sense, this makes his father, who is responsible for his poverty, also responsible for his arrest. But it is the other detail, the fact that the charge is arson, and the fact that there has been 'so much destruction of property that way lately' (103) which is more significant, because according to Keith Snell in his *Annals of the Labouring Poor*,

> as late as the 1880s and 1890s there was so much arson in some areas of Dorset that it was reported, and later recalled by elderly labourers, that many young men dared not go out in the evenings for fear of being accused as arsonists.[18]

And behind that note lie the facts of a rural society that was in such a depressed state that, to quote from Snell again, 'from Tolpuddle on throughout the nineteenth century, in literary and blue book reportage, the Dorset agricultural labourer was associated with about the most squalid and depressed living standards to be found in England, and the most embittered class relations'.[19] All this is only squinted at in the story; what Hardy is scrupulous about is recording the effects of the dominant ideologies upon the lives of his characters, and this is built into the fabric of the texts of *The Mayor of Casterbridge* and of 'The Withered Arm'. What he approaches in a much more clandestine fashion – what he evidently has misgivings about coming to terms with – is a full disclosure of the actual living conditions that his stories only partly divulge. It is the social history which can just be glimpsed through those breaches in the fabric, such as the reference to arson in the 1880s, that emerges, only to be encrypted, in *Wessex Tales* as a whole.[20]

This encryption, or even deflection from, the extremely harsh realities of agricultural poverty and injustice in Dorset is evident when one juxtaposes the story of the unnamed boy hanged at the close of 'The Withered Arm' with a tale that Hardy recounted to Newman Flower:

> My father saw four men hung for *being with* some others who had set fire to a rick. Among them was a stripling of a boy of eighteen. Skinny. Half-starved. So frail, so underfed, that they had to put weights on his feet to break his neck. He had not fired the rick. But with a youth's excitement he had rushed to the scene of the blaze [. . .]. Nothing my father ever said to me drove the tragedy of Life so deeply into my mind.[21]

Hardy must be ranked among the great tragic writers of the Victorian period, and this gives his statement that nothing 'drove the tragedy of Life so deeply into my mind' considerable weight and importance. Yet Hardy never directly used the dreadful details of his father's reminiscence, but rather deflected the facts in a variety of turnings or tropes from its harsh realities. In his tale, 'The Winters and the Palmleys' from *Life's Little Ironies*, Hardy's turning from his father's account lies not in the physical details of the execution, but in the crime and its motivation: Jack is sentenced for the night burglary of his own love letters, written to a scornful lover who refuses to return them to him. He feels exposed to her contempt because the letters are semi-literate, and he is desperate to get them back. Harriet, the haughty former lover, is influenced by her aunt to fail to come to his defence, and the aunt in turn has exerted this influence as she has an old feud with Jack's widowed mother who 'stole' her lover in years past, and who she also feels is responsible for the death of her own small son many years before. Thus the causes leading to Jack's execution are entirely couched in two generations of personal relations which include sexual rivalry, social envy, maternal bereavement and romantic rejection. These are removed from the political upheavals that his father remembered when, as in 'The Withered Arm' the boy was executed for suspected rick-burning (although even here, the boy's semi-literacy and the harsh sentence he receives point to social injustice and neglect). Although 'The Withered Arm' is 'sensational' in its use of the supernatural, Hardy avoids using the sensational details his father related. While the social history is in place, related to Gertrude by a hangman who is actually sympathetic to his next 'customer', the execution happens at a distance, focalised mainly through Gertrude. She waits for the body of the hanged man in a room inside the prison and does not see the execution at all, but only hears the 'babble' of the multitudes and 'the hoarse croak of a single voice uttering the words, "Last dying speech and confession!"' (105). What that speech or confession is we never hear; there is no access to the interiority, the individuality of the unnamed hanged boy. When the body is brought in, it is referred to as a 'corpse', a 'burden', a 'dead man'. It is only when Rhoda Brook enters and shrieks to Gertrude, 'Hussy – to come between us and our child now!' (106) that the corpse suddenly becomes someone's child – still unnamed, as he has been throughout the story – but now related, part of the tale and an individual who was very young, vulnerable and who suffered injustice.

In 'The Winters and the Palmleys' the physical details of the hanging witnessed by Hardy's father are adhered to: young Jack Winter

> was so boyish and slim that they were obliged in mercy to hang him in the heaviest fetters kept in the jail, lest his heft should not break his neck, and they weighed so upon him that he could hardly drag himself to the drop. (*Life's Little Ironies*, 245)

This last detail, supplied by Hardy, of the boy's physical disability in having to drag himself to his own death powerfully evokes the terrible vulnerability, helplessness and exposure of the boy, staged before hundreds if not thousands of onlookers. Execution stories often seem to focus on these small physical, sometimes practical details: just as Jack

Winter could hardly drag himself to the scaffold, so Lady Jane Grey famously cried for help to find the block as, blindfolded, she groped helplessly to get to it. Mary Stuart's dismembered head was held aloft after her 1587 execution, only to roll onto the floor as the head came away from the wig she had worn, horribly exposing her dead body as spectacle, and also exposing her memory to the taunts of those who reviled her as vain and duplicitous. Hardy's own ingrained memory from boyhood of Martha Browne's execution is similarly preoccupied with physical detail: in his eighties he recalled her 'fine figure' hanging in a 'misty rain' which helped the 'tight black silk gown set off her shape'.[22] Certainly the memory has sexual overtones, as Robert Gittings has argued, but it is also an image which emphasises her spectacular vulnerability and exposure.

Similarly, in 'The Withered Arm', it is the seemingly inconsequential physical details in this execution story which are so powerful, and which stand in for or act as Hardy's artistic deflections away from the more sensational details of the weights on the boy's half-starved body in Thomas Hardy Senior's story. Hardy writes that 'the corpse had been thrown into the coffin so hastily that the skirt of the smockfrock was hanging over' (106). There is of course a haste and lack of respect for the body of the boy, as he has been 'thrown' into the coffin. There is also a tremendous vulnerability about the executed person, as he or she is subjected to the gaze, but is no longer able to compose the body or dress before public scrutiny. The skirt hanging over the coffin's edge, in a similar if less dramatic way than in the case of Martha Browne's black silk dress or Mary Stuart's wig, emphasises the boy's powerlessness and exposure to indignity in death.

The smockfrock would also have indicated to many among Hardy's urban readership that the boy was a farm labourer, a member of that class called 'Hodge'. Hardy wrote in 'The Dorsetshire Labourer', an article for the *Longman's Magazine* in 1883, how the 'caricature' of Hodge was too often 'taken as truth' by a readership unfamiliar with the agricultural world: 'Thus when we arrive at the farm-labouring community we find it to be seriously personified by the pitiable picture known as Hodge; not only so, but the community is assumed to be a uniform collection of concrete Hodges'.[23] In 1880 Leslie Stephen interestingly made the mistake about uniform Hodges that Hardy so deplored. Encouraging him to write a collection of short stories, he recommended that Hardy apply himself to some 'prose-idylls of country life – short sketches of Hodge & his ways'.[24] This recommendation eventually resulted in *Wessex Tales*, but in this collection Hardy is clearly addressing and vilifying the process and perspective that can turn an impoverished, neglected and unnamed boy into merely another 'Hodge'.

The boy's body is exposed after execution to those who may read or interpret his existence as belonging to that of a criminal, a Hodge or a beloved son. Written upon his flesh is the hangman's mark around his neck, 'a line the colour of an unripe blackberry'. Hardy makes it clear that from the time this boy was very young, he and his mother had survived by his poaching; they would most certainly have needed what they could pick from the hedgerows as well. The reference to blackberries reminds us that Rhoda and her son lived on the edge of survival, an atavistic existence in their remote cottage which relied upon hunting and gathering. It was that or die of starvation, and a memory which most probably informs this depiction of Rhoda and her son's impoverishment is that of a local boy whom Hardy was horrified to hear of in his own boyhood, who had died of starvation. When an autopsy was conducted, they found only raw turnip in his stomach, most probably filched from a farmer's field.[25]

When Conjuror Trendle examines Gertrude's shrivelled arm, he tells her: 'This is of the nature of a blight, not of the nature of a wound' (93). A wound is inflicted once, but blight is a disease and can be spread. This is exactly the nature of the markings on Gertrude's arm. The blight takes the form of a hand grasped there, and both Gertrude and Rhoda come to believe that it is the supernatural imprint of Rhoda's hand. Hands were considered extremely revealing indicators of personality, class and sensibility in the nineteenth century: small, delicate hands signified the qualities of a lady; casts of women's and children's hands were taken to be sculpted in marble and displayed in the upper-class home. Rhoda is obsessed with Gertrude's looks and especially with her hands. Before she has ever seen her rival, she asks her son to see whether Gertrude 'shows marks of the lady on her' (71), and this is specifically focused: 'notice if her hands be white; if not, see if they look as though she had ever done housework, or are milker's hands like mine' (71). Rhoda's hands are marked with signs of poverty and labour, so it is appropriate that the mark of the blight that she conveys to Gertrude be a hand; it passes something of the neglect and injustices she has been dealt onto her rival's unsullied flesh. But in fact all the characters in the story are marked, and the marks and impressions they receive are conveyed from one to another as a blight or disease. Rhoda is marked and her body withered by labour. She is also stigmatised in the community because she has an illegitimate child. This marking and setting apart is the result of Lodge's neglect and injustice to her. Her mark is passed onto Gertrude in the form of the withered arm, and it is implied that this disfigurement sexually repels Lodge, rendering his marriage childless.

Thinking of Rhoda and her son, Lodge 'fear[s] this might be a judgment from heaven upon him' (91); as the initiator of this blight of injustice, he feels marked out by God for retributive justice. Indeed, like Barnet's face in 'Fellow-Townsmen', the preceding story of *Wessex Tales*, Lodge's countenance is 'lined', and his character altered by the pain of watching his only child hanged. Even the 'soft and evanescent' Gertrude is able to leave her mark: her beauty 'had evidently made an impression even on the somewhat hard nature of the boy' (72, 75).

Gertrude's unnamed son acts as a sort of conductor for both supernatural and natural energies (of sexual rivalry, bitterness over neglect, loneliness) which connect and blight Lodge, Rhoda and Gertrude. After all, it is his existence which is the cause and the symbol of Lodge's initial injustice to Rhoda. The boy's sustained gaze at Gertrude's face in full sunlight enabled him to convey to his mother an image of her rival as 'realistic as a photograph' enabling her unconsciously to produce the imprint of a hand upon Gertrude's arm, very much like a photographic negative. His role, then, as a conductor of these energies, makes it entirely appropriate that his body become the site at which these marked and blighted characters meet. Gertrude seeks to cure her withered arm by a 'turn of the blood' which will result, presumably, from the shock of placing her limb against something which is alien and dramatically different from her own disfigurement. But she cannot know that the line of the hangman's rope on the boy's neck and her own marked limb arise from the same source – from the injustice that has been passed on in the 'nature of a blight, not of the nature of a wound' between all the characters gathered in the prison room. Like the repellent energy between two like magnetic forces, the shock that kills Gertrude arises from the intensity of the meeting of two like marks.

Hardy's allusions to photography and to galvanism in 'The Withered Arm' may at first seem an attempt to offer a scientific explanation of the story's supernatural occurrences. In fact the rationalist Leslie Stephen urged Hardy to provide an explanation for the 'overlooking' and withering of the arm – either that or to 'hint that you tell the story as somebody told it' (that is to say, as an unreliable Hodge told it to him).[26] Hardy does neither, but produces a sophisticated narrator whose authoritative statement that ' "the turn of the blood," predicted by the conjuror, had taken place' discourages incredulity or challenge (106). The allusions to science are not simply there to 'address themselves to a Victorian audience' and to establish the difference in timeframe between the setting of the story and its telling.[27] Instead, they offer much insight into the complex position of the story's narrator as well as highlighting the somewhat indefinite lines of demarcation between science and superstition.

In trying to pluck up the courage to go through with Conjuror Trendle's suggested counter-spell, the terrified Gertrude considers that the words of the Conjuror: ' "It will turn your blood" [could be] seen to be capable of a scientific no less than a ghastly interpretation' (95). The possibility of the cure being in some way scientifically wrought helps her to cope with the fact that the superstitious remedy she seeks goes against all the teachings of her school-girl days, and also helps her to overcome the fear of her husband's fury were he to find out that she was embarking upon this remedy: 'She dared not tell him, for she had found by delicate experiment that these smouldering village beliefs made him furious if mentioned, partly because he half entertained them himself' (96). Clearly the belief in or dismissal of these village beliefs is related to class, education and social mobility. Farmer Lodge is upwardly mobile, and this trajectory is part of the reason that he has wed the fairly well-educated daughter of a wealthy farmer, rather than Rhoda Brook, his own dairymaid. Like Michael Henchard, who makes a secret visit to Conjuror Fell in *The Mayor of Casterbridge*, he is ashamed of his own smouldering beliefs.

The references to photography act as a scientific frame upon the process of 'overlooking'. As discussed, the rapt, extended stare at Gertrude by Rhoda's boy is in obedience to his mother's bidding that he 'give her a look'. As with a sitter for a photographic portrait at this time, Gertrude's exposure to the boy's gaze has to be sustained to sufficiently develop the image. In both photography and in the overlooking process in which the boy is unconsciously participating, light is essential: 'The low sun was full in her face, rendering every feature, shade, and contour distinct, from the curve of her little nostril to the colour of her eyes' (73). The boy's mind is imprinted with this image and this is conveyed back to his mother: 'from her boy's description and the casual words of the other milkers, Rhoda Brook would raise a mental image of the unconscious Mrs Lodge that was realistic as a photograph' (76). These words end the second episode of the story; the third begins again with light working to produce an image, as Rhoda stares into the fire immediately upon her retiring: 'She contemplated so intently the new wife, as presented to her in her mind's eye over the embers, that she forgot the lapse of time' (77). That night the incubus of a fiendish Mrs Lodge visits Rhoda and she imprints the shape of a hand onto Gertrude's arm. Kristin Brady has interestingly discussed how Gertrude and Rhoda 'can be seen as similar or complementary, even while they are diametrically opposed [. . .] they are like different views of one image.'[28] In fact, they are very like a photograph and its negative: Rhoda (her name from the Greek meaning 'rose'), and Gertrude, represented by the paler shades 'like the light under a heap of rose petals', acknowledge their similarities and a growing closeness to each other, but Rhoda's dark eyes, hair and outlook on life constitute a 'negative' image of obscurity and shade, while Gertrude's light eyes, hair and skin and her corresponding sunny disposition have been able to develop under bright aspects.

The scientific process of photography and the supernatural process of overlooking are juxtaposed in this story in order to question some of the rationalist assertions made by Leslie Stephen, Farmer Lodge and all who believe that they have risen above superstitious beliefs by virtue of their class and education. The science behind photography was believed in by many Victorians, but most probably took the science on faith rather than really understood it (indeed, for some the process seemed magical). Overlooking may be a superstition, but there is no more reason to dismiss it because it is not understood, than there is to dismiss the science behind photography: such at least is the stance implied by a sophisticated narrator who gives credence to Conjuror Trendle's advice. While using educated language, familiar with the scientific development of the day, he refuses to distance himself from the supernatural aspects of the tale by putting it into the words of an unrealistic 'Hodge', as Leslie Stephen suggested. After all, the 'aged friend' who related the story to Hardy (as he writes in the Preface to *Wessex Tales*) was most probably his mother, and Hardy was never going to think of her as unreliable or as a simple Hodge (vi). The social distance between Leslie Stephen and Hardy is sharply focused here. Stephen's obtuse comments demonstrate his failure to comprehend that Hardy was immersed imaginatively in folk customs and superstitions, that for him they were very close to home, and that he realised that they gave a power and force otherwise denied to the impoverished and oppressed in rural 'Wessex'.

While Leslie Stephen advised Hardy to position the 'The Withered Arm' as a second-hand and, by implication, unreliable telling, Kristin Brady again raised this vexed issue of the untrustworthy narrator just over a century later. She claimed of another story from *Wessex Tales*, that 'the correct interpretation of this second story requires a recognition that its narrator is not reliable'.[29] Of this story, 'A Tradition of Eighteen Hundred and Four', she concludes that it is 'a depiction of the possible falseness of the oral tale, which depends so heavily not only on the honesty but also on the clearheadedness of its sources.'[30] This assessment does not speak to the complexity of the narratorial stance in Hardy's writing generally – and more specifically in the short stories which are so close to orally-transmitted tales. The two 'Napoleonic' stories in *Wessex Tales* – 'A Tradition of Eighteen Hundred and Four' and 'The Melancholy Hussar of the German Legion' (henceforth, 'The

Melancholy Hussar') – were both transferred to this volume from *Life's Little Ironies* in 1912. The stories stand apart in *Wessex Tales* because they are Napoleonic, because they both are told by an identifiable frame narrator and also because they are constructed by a layering of narrators, one giving way to another. This layering produces a Chinese-box effect which has at its core the seeming dichotomies of oral versus written, invention versus truth, and also the presence or the distance of the narrator. These are all crucial issues for Hardy, as he is fixing these transmutable oral tales in written form.

'A Tradition of Eighteen Hundred and Four' (henceforth 'A Tradition') was written in 1882 for the annual *Harper's Christmas*, and it exhibits many of the expected features of a Christmas story: it is meant to give a *frisson* of fear to those within the story who are sheltering from the rain and cold by the inn fireside, and also to the readers of the periodical sitting by the Christmas hearth. A frame narrator remembers a story told more than ten years ago when he gathered around the inn fire with the other locals. The narrative, then given over to Solomon Selby and told in the first person, tells of how as a child he was sent to keep watch over the ewes one winter night. His uncle, a soldier, came with him and together, sheltering in a heap of straw, they witnessed Napoleon and another French soldier looking over a map of the Channel and surveying the surrounding landscape and coast for a good invasion landing-place. It was a period when Dorset and the coastal areas of 'Wessex' came to national importance in the guard against invasion, and also a time of fear and vulnerability: as Solomon Selby says, if Napoleon had landed in Lulworth Cove, 'we coast-folk should have been cut down one and all, and I should not have sat here to tell this tale' (40). Instead of the traditional Christmas ghost, Hardy gives us the 'Corsican Ogre', Napoleon. The young boy of the story sees Napoleon's face, lit suddenly by a lantern on a lonely downland in the dead of night. While the terror and excitement that this inspires in the boy is highly appropriate for the Christmas ghost-story genre, it also serves to immerse readers in the highly-charged atmosphere of this period – its fascination with Napoleon and fear of his invasion.

Hardy's preoccupation with the Napoleonic era lasted from boyhood to old age. Correcting the final proofs of his Napoleonic epic *The Dynasts* in late 1907, he wrote that he felt 'like an old Campaigner – just as if I had been present at the Peninsular battles & Waterloo (as they say Geo. IV imagined of himself)'.[31] Indeed, it is presence itself which is so exciting and urgent here: the presence of Selby, 'sat here'; Hardy's own imaginative presence at the scene of battle; the presence of local people who remembered the time. He values tremendously what he realises is the last chance to be in the presence of those who were present then. Faithful and frequent visits over the years to chat with the Chelsea pensioners who had fought at Waterloo attests to this. In 1875, for example, on the sixtieth anniversary of Waterloo, Hardy and his wife Emma visited the old Waterloo pensioners still surviving in the Chelsea Hospital and listened to the stories of John Bentley, 'a delightful old campaigner' whom Hardy 'knew to the last' (*Life*, 109). Bentley related stories to Emma of the battle, but also of a romance he fondly remembered with a Belgian woman just before Waterloo. Even in the journal entry quoted in the *Life*, one can sense the pleasure of being in the presence of this man, his arm around Emma's waist, the captivation of oral storytelling, but also Hardy's urgent desire to catch the details of his stories – to get them right – so that they can be recorded and not forgotten (*Life*, 109). Hardy listened to the reminiscences of those of his parents' and grandparents' generations in his local area, and his notes in the *Life* give ample evidence of how those tales found a refracted and sometimes direct form in his own writing. They appeal to him in every sense of the word because they are set in a time that is just slipping out of living memory.

The Napoleonic Wars brought rural, isolated corners of 'Wessex' into dramatic contact with the wider world. At the opening of Hardy's story 'The Fiddler of the Reels' he writes of the Great Exhibition having acted as a sort of 'geological fault' by which layers representing widely disparate periods of time (those of Regency, or even medieval Wessex and modern London) were made suddenly contiguous. The Wars brought different cultures and the time periods they inhabited together in similarly abrupt fashion. Solomon Selby, the narrator of 'A Tradition', has lived in an area of about four square miles all his life, but he can recount admirably a history of Napoleon's battles across 'the great Alp mountains', Egypt, Turkey, Austria and Prussia. This foreign history does not make Napoleon a remote figure; he is 'Neighbour Boney', and even before the boy Selby sees Bonaparte in his father's ewe-lease, his father had 'seen' him on the coast of France:

> My father drove a flock of ewes up into Sussex that year, and as he went along the drovers' track over the high downs thereabout he could see this drilling [of Napoleon's troops] actually going on – the accoutrements of the rank and file glittering in the sun like silver. (34–5)

In the two Napoleonic stories of *Wessex Tales*, the foreign and exotic are almost on the doorstep (in the case of 'The Melancholy Hussar', literally so). This meeting of the foreign and the local produces storytellers of great power. Selby can stop all conversation with his 'narrative smile', and inspire belief by his 'manner' and narrative presence.

Walter Benjamin isolated two types of storyteller from 'the many nameless' whose tales had been passed along the generations: there is the storyteller who 'has come from afar' to fascinate with exotic adventures, and there is 'the man who has stayed at home, making an honest living, and who knows the local tales and traditions.'[32] He goes on to claim that, 'the actual extension of the realm of storytelling in its full historical breadth is inconceivable without the most intimate interpenetration of these two archaic types.'[33] Both Solomon Selby and the soldier Matthäus Tina of 'The Melancholy Hussar' have achieved this interpenetration of the far and near, the exotic and homely.

This narratorial stance, this interpenetration, has to be important for Hardy as he travels between London and Dorset, relating stories to an urban readership of rural customs and traditions which to them may seem remote, exotic, from a far-away time and place, but which to him are local and familiar. Equally, from the perspective of his home, he is the man who has travelled, the native who has returned, to tell stories. This is part of the reason why the narratorial voice in much of Hardy's writing seems oddly distanced, slightly uninvolved. As Hillis Miller has written, 'Almost every sentence Hardy ever wrote, whether in his fiction, in his poetry, or in his more private writings, is objective. It names something outside the mind of which that mind is aware.'[34] While Hillis Miller discusses other crucial reasons for what he calls Hardy's 'refusal of involvement' (some of which we will discuss in our consideration of the story 'Fellow-Townsmen'), it is also the case that, like Tess Durbeyfield, Hardy's narrators often speak 'two languages': like Benjamin's ideal storyteller, they speak of the near and far, and this interpenetration raises a quandary in that they can never be fully immersed or involved in either place.

This project of storytelling from the perspective of the near and far raises a dilemma for Hardy about the disparate nature of oral and written tales, and this difficulty is evident in his Preface to *Wessex Tales*. There he writes of the composition of 'The Withered Arm' that he has been 'reminded' by an 'aged friend who knew "Rhoda Brook" ' that the incubus appeared, not in the dead of night, as in the story, but while she was 'lying down on a hot afternoon'. Hardy continues:

> To my mind the occurrence of such a vision in the daytime is more impressive than if it had happened in a midnight dream. Readers are therefore asked to correct the misrelation, which affords an instance of how our imperfect memories insensibly formalize the fresh originality of living fact – from whose shape they slowly depart, as machine-made castings depart by degrees from the sharp hand-work of the mould. (vi)

Hardy's metaphor for how stories diverge from the original tale through the 'imperfect memories' of the storyteller is odd. The 'machine-made castings' he writes of would seem more appropriate to the technology of print culture, rather than the cumulative, organic processes of oral transmission across generations. He often insisted that his stories were true, told to him first-hand by the protagonist, or second- or third-hand by someone who knew the original characters involved. His anxiety to submit the 'true story' to the written record would seem to support Kristin Brady's assertion, quoted earlier, that 'A Tradition' is, 'a depiction of the possible falseness of the oral tale, which depends so heavily not only on the honesty but also on the clear-headedness of its sources.'[35] Neither Brady's comment, nor Hardy's metaphor of 'machine-made castings' fits well with Walter Benjamin's description of the oral story or 'the artisan form of communication'. Benjamin writes of the story:

> It does not aim to convey the pure essence of the thing, like information or a report. It sinks the thing into the life of the storyteller, in order to bring it out of him again. Thus traces of the storyteller cling to the story the way the handprints of the potter cling to the clay vessel.[36]

The trouble is that Benjamin's description is so evocative of Hardy's writing. As in the second stanza of his poem 'Old Furniture':

> I see the hands of the generations
> That owned each shiny familiar thing
> In play on its knobs and indentations
> And with its ancient fashioning
> Still dallying:[37]

While in the last stanza of the poem Hardy concedes regretfully, 'The world has no use for one today / Who eyes things thus', he is, after all, 'a man who used to notice such things' ('Afterwards').[38] Paths across downland, marked out by centuries of travellers walking there, the patina of familiar homely objects created by 'hands behind hands' ('Old Furniture'), or the generations of storytellers who leave their 'handprints' on the story: all this layering is crucial to Hardy's writing and his idiosyncratic narratorial stance as he negotiates oral and written culture. In these two Napoleonic stories then, the presence of the narrator is important, as it is a way of crossing the divide between oral and written tales: being in the presence of a narrator who was present at the time of the story's action, or who knew the protagonist, is a way of getting at the original 'living fact' which Hardy wants to excavate before he gives the tale written form. But presence also conveys the pleasure Hardy takes in the individuality of the storyteller, in his particularity, idiosyncrasy and therefore in his ability to embellish the tale with the mark of personality. Embellishment and literal truth are of course at odds, and this dilemma is evident in different aspects of the two Napoleonic tales.

Solomon Selby has a narrative presence so powerful that it is second only to 'the direct testimony of [the reader's] own eyes'. Hardy is at pains to create an atmosphere of truth and presence in the tale: both Selby and the frame narrator scorn the 'incredulity of the age' (40) which has resulted in the tale being 'seldom repeated', because too unbelievable, and Selby dismisses those 'makers of newspapers', 'printers of books' and 'gentry who only believe what they see in printed lines' (36). Oral culture is clearly antagonistic to print culture here. Yet for all the persuasive protestations of the layered narrators, Hardy admitted in a note to the 1919 edition of *Wessex Tales* that the story was pure 'invention'. A number of critics have commented upon this invention, and especially upon Hardy's various responses to the possibility that his tale had given rise to a belief that Napoleon's visit to the Dorset coast was an actual oral tradition – perhaps true. As Kathryn King has commented:

> The Hardy who 'instituted inquiries to correct tricks of memory' in order to set down for his 'own satisfaction a fairly true record of a vanishing life'[39] would doubtless be chagrined to think that he had himself introduced another contaminant from print culture into the oral world and thus muddied such pools of oral culture as still remained in an increasingly print-orientated Wessex.[40]

As Martin Ray notes, it could well have been Herbert Trench's play *Napoleon*, staged in London in 1919, which prompted Hardy to investigate whether or not the tradition at the centre of his invented story was true. (The play had treated the story as fact.) Hardy wrote to thank Sydney Cockerell for investigating whether or not there was an historical basis for the tradition, or whether it was a 'tradition' at all, or one implanted by Hardy's story:

> It would certainly be very strange if an invented story should turn out to have already existed [. . .]. What you may be sure of is that I never heard of any such tradition. It may be that my having, with the licence of a storyteller to tell lies, *pretended* there was such an account in being, led people to think there was. Of course I did it to give verisimilitude to *my* story.[41]

Hardy is perfectly straightforward here that a storyteller in either written or oral culture, 'tells lies', embellishes and invents. Part of the 'truth' of Hardy's 'A Tradition' lies in the pleasure taken by the frame narrator and in turn by the readers of the tale in the power of Solomon Selby to inspire belief. But it is nevertheless the case that this story led Hardy to question his 'license to tell lies' in some circumstances. As he wrote in the *Life* concerning this tale:

> A curious question arose in Hardy's mind at this date on whether a romancer was morally justified in going to extreme lengths of assurance – after the manner of Defoe – in respect of a tale he knew to be absolutely false. (*Life*, 424)

It may be that Hardy is personally engaged with this question and that of the adulteration of the oral by written culture in this story especially, because of the background to the development of the character of Solomon Selby. Selby was most probably based in part upon James Selby of Broadmayne, Dorset, a man who is mentioned (but not named) in the Preface to *Wessex Tales* as having been in 'my father's employ for over thirty years'. Hardy gives him credit for much of the very detailed information about smuggling, used in the last story of *Wessex Tales*, 'The Distracted Preacher'. But Selby is also mentioned in the *Life* as an informant for 'The Melancholy Hussar': he is the man who thought he could point out the mark on Bincombe Down where the German soldiers were shot. Hardy must have listened to James Selby's stories from boyhood, and he can take him to that most evocative place for the writer – a human mark on the landscape. Selby has given evidence for a story in which, as Hardy adds to the above entry, 'the real names of the deserters' were given; so, a story which he knew to have a factual basis. Possibly Hardy's various comments about the invention of tradition involved in 'A Tradition of Eighteen Hundred and Four' reveal a concern that he has in some ways betrayed the trust of the many, often aged, oral storytellers and informants who spoke to him over the years. If Solomon Selby is a fictive version of James Selby, who gave much detailed historical information to Hardy, then the placing of a total invention in Selby's mouth may have seemed a more personal act of bad faith than he could be entirely comfortable with. However Hardy does celebrate the presence and power of these storytellers, and possibly aligns himself with Solomon Selby in producing a story which he has the power to make people believe true. His ambivalence over invention, over how far he can justify calling his tales true, and how he uses the stories of oral informers are all indicators of his dilemma over oral and written culture – a dilemma which is addressed but not solved in 'A Tradition'.

Both Napoleonic stories in *Wessex* Tales are constituted by layers of storytellers. 'A Tradition' begins with the frame narrator, who introduces Selby, and Selby includes in his tale the fascinating storytelling powers of his soldier uncle, Job. 'The Melancholy Hussar' is related by a narrator who, in his boyhood, listened to Phyllis Grove tell her story exclusively to him. The romance of her tale rests partly on her Desdemona-like enthralment by the stories of another solider, Matthäus Tina of the York Hussars. Hardy emulates the process of oral transmission in written form in these stories. He attempts to make presence felt, and to make the stamp or mark of each storyteller, as it is layered over the next, one that is vivid and uneffaced.

Clearly there were moments of doubt when Hardy felt that past stories, events, sensations could not be resuscitated, become vivid to a reader's or listener's mind. In a journal entry from January 1897, included in the *Life*, he wrote, 'Today has length, breadth, thickness, colour, smell, voice. As soon as it becomes *yesterday* it is a thin layer among many layers, without substance, colour or articulate sound' (*Life*, 302). Walter Benjamin writes of the oral tradition as 'that slow piling one on top of the other of thin, transparent layers which constitutes the most appropriate picture of the way in which the perfect narrative is revealed through the layers of a variety of retellings'.[42] Hardy's writing is haunted by the problem that the human mark will be erased forever: whether it is the mark on the landscape, the name on a grave, the distinctiveness of each layer of storyteller, or layer of yesterdays as in his journal entry, he writes to fend off the moment of erasure. Even in his everyday life, he carried a little brush in his pocket in old age to clean inscriptions on gravestones, brushing off the layers of dirt and moss until the name and the grave's narrative was restored. Sophie Gilmartin has argued elsewhere about how Hardy's use of colour, voice and sensation belies the sentiments of his journal entry above,[43] and the opening paragraph of 'The Melancholy Hussar' is a good example of his characteristic attempt to defeat time with intense sensory perceptions:

> Here stretch the downs, high and breezy and green, absolutely unchanged since those eventful days. A plough has never disturbed the turf, and the sod that was uppermost then is uppermost now. Here stood the camp; here are distinct traces of the banks thrown up for the horses of the cavalry, and spots where the midden-heaps lay are still to be observed. At night, when I walk across the lonely place, it is impossible to avoid hearing, amid the scourings of the wind over the grass-bents and thistles, the old trumpet and bugle calls, the rattle of the halters; to help seeing rows of spectral tents and the *impedimenta* of the soldiery. From within the canvases come guttural syllables of foreign tongues and broken songs of the fatherland; for they were mainly regiments of the King's German Legion that slept round the tent-poles hereabout at that time. (45)

The passage is permeated by the sensual. The first-person narrator who walks across the lonely downland is very much present and addresses the reader directly as he makes 'length, breadth, thickness, colour, smell, voice' substantial, articulate and of the present moment, even though as he says, the story took place 'nearly ninety years ago'. Indeed the narrator of this story is peculiarly meticulous about the time that the heroine, Phyllis Grove, told her story to him: 'She was then an old lady of seventy-five, and her auditor a lad of fifteen' (46). He goes on that she lived twelve years after telling him the story, and at the time of his recounting it she has been dead 'nearly twenty' years. Hardy enjoins his reader to do the maths, and the calculations make the narrator the same age that Hardy was when he first began the story, probably in the early summer of 1888. He seems to align himself with this story's narrator, if not to absolutely identify with him, and this does give the tale a markedly personal and oral quality. The opening phrase, 'Here stretch the downs', places the reader alongside the narrator in that place and moment. In fact Hardy admitted that 'The Melancholy Hussar' had a personal interest for him and a 'hold' upon him,

> for the technically inadmissible reasons that the old people who gave me their recollections of its incidents did so in circumstances that linger pathetically in the memory; that she who, at the age of ninety, pointed out the unmarked resting-place of the two soldiers in the tale, was probably the last remaining eyewitness of their death and interment . . . [44]

As mentioned earlier, one of the first references to the story is the journal entry of 1877, when James Selby thought there was 'a mark' on the downs where the soldiers were executed. In 1896, Hardy wrote in a letter to Bertram Windle that the soldiers 'were shot where the roads cross' on 'Bincombe Down'.[45] Clearly, for Hardy and for Hardy's narrator, marks on the physical landscape of Wessex are important because they corroborate the truth of the tale. However the story itself is really concerned with 'unmarked resting-places' and human tracks and traces on the down which are the most ephemeral and minute. Phyllis Grove has been conducting a romance from across the boundary garden wall of her father's isolated manor house, with a German soldier of the York Hussars. The soldier, who is encamped on the down with his regiment, first sees Phyllis while walking the downland path that passes under the wall. Late in the story, after many and increasingly intimate conversations engaged in across this boundary, Phyllis crosses the garden probably for the last time:

> She observed that her frequent visits to this corner had quite trodden down the grass in the angle of the wall, and left marks of garden soil on the stepping-stones by which she had mounted to look over the top. Seldom having gone there till dusk, she had not considered that her traces might be visible by day. Perhaps it was these which had revealed her trysts to her father. (63)

Hardy's novels and short stories often follow or view people as they walk: from Gaymead to London, as does Sam in 'The Fiddler of the Reels'; to Talbothays, as does Tess, glimpsed from a bird's-eye view as she walks across a large expanse of downland, appearing 'like a fly on a billiard-table'; along the endlessly long Long-Ash Lane, as does Marty South from *The Woodlanders*, and characters from 'Interlopers at the Knap'; into Casterbridge, as do Elizabeth-Jane and her mother. Whether for migrant workers on the tramp, or a gentleman like Barnet in 'Fellow-Townsmen' taking the air, there is a sense of spaciousness and purposive energy inspired by the Wessex landscape: its ancient paths have been worn by so many, each with some desire or purpose, that it invites movement across it. Occasionally, however, Hardy describes a character, usually a woman, who is utterly circumscribed in a tiny space, such as the lame Sophy Twycott in 'The Son's Veto' (from *Life's Little Ironies*) or even Lizzy Newberry of 'The Distracted Preacher' if her fate should take her from night-roving over the downs and cliffs to 'correctness of conduct and a minister's parlour in some far-removed inland county' (258).

Phyllis Grove of 'The Melancholy Hussar' is one of the most confined of Hardy's women, perhaps even more so than Sophy Twycott. Her father, a 'professional man', has tired of the world and retreated to a small manor house high on a lonely down. At one point in the story he orders his daughter never to leave the garden, accusing her of 'walking' with a soldier. Phyllis knows it is 'useless for her to protest that she had never taken a walk with any soldier or man under the sun except [her father]' (57). She does very little walking anywhere in this extremely claustrophobic story. Her father's gloom and embitterment make her home unhappy and constraining and the only place she is allowed to go is to her aunt's which is a 'prison' to her (57). The little, ephemeral path that she beats to the garden's boundary wall takes her to 'the only inch of English ground in which she took any interest' (63), but her daily walk there is not now for any prospect it might give her of distant sea or downland (although it was when she was a confined child) but because it is the place where Matthäus Tina meets her and tells her stories of his homeland in Saarbrück.

The soldier is a great storyteller who, like Benjamin's ideal, interpenetrates the near and far, exotic and homely in his tales, and Phyllis, 'Like Desdemona, pitied him, and learnt his history' (51). He tells her tales of his home, foreign to her, but his telling communicates a love of his 'native place' and succeeds in making the exotic familiar to her. Because she is 'not a native of the village, like all the joyous girls around her', she finally feels far more connected to Tina's home than to Wessex. He 'had infected her with his own passionate longing for his country, and mother, and home' (56).

The male narrator of the story is highly attentive to the physical and spectral Wessex landscape and the human marks traced upon it. He freely roams across this space and has a love for its local stories and traditions, but he relates a story that centres upon two people who do not care at all for Wessex or indeed for England. While Tina is a good storyteller partly because of his passion for his home country, his immersion in the local, Phyllis fails as a storyteller because she is so alienated from her locality and her kind. Although she is engaged to be married, her fiancé has neglected her entirely and she no longer believes he will marry her. Her father is remote and 'unkind' and there is no-one else to connect her to the world, other than the soldier. By the time she tells her story to the narrator as a boy, she is an old woman, and her life-long disconnection from the local has meant that she has never been able to tell her own story properly, to explain herself. This has resulted in 'rumours' and 'fragments of her story' being told 'which are precisely those which are most unfavourable to her character' (46).

Phyllis's escape from her home, down the road towards the coast, is one of only two occasions that we see her outside the garden boundary. When Gould, her neglectful fiancé, returns upon the night of her planned elopement she mistakenly assumes that he is come to keep faith with her after all, and she is therefore appalled that she had considered escape with the man she loves. She returns home to be dutiful. Her second journey beyond the garden wall occurs the following morning when she walks out with Gould. In one of Hardy's terrible ironies of mistiming, Gould confesses to her that he has secretly married another, and asks Phyllis to smooth the matter over for him by saying she could not have married him. Phyllis realises that she could have eloped with impunity the night before, but now, as is so often the case in Hardy's writings, it is too late. Preparing for her walk with Gould the morning after her parting from Tina, Phyllis 'was in that wretched state of mind which leads a woman to move mechanically onward in what she conceives to be her allotted path' (61). Several days after Gould and Matthäus Tina have left, she notices the little path that she has made before the boundary wall. She climbs the wall which lies above the downland path where Tina had walked to meet her, only to watch in horror as her soldier and his comrade are shot for desertion in the distance at a spot 'where the roads meet', on the down where Selby had told Hardy there was a 'mark'. Paths, roads, places of execution, graves, all mark the landscape of this story, as they do in Hardy's writing generally, but the very small distances between these sites in 'The Melancholy Hussar' tend to intensify their force and their evocative energy for the characters and for the reader.

J. Hillis Miller has written of space in Hardy as a 'continuum' in which, 'people in their relations to one another have the power to traverse space in real movement or in imagination and to create thereby a complex structure of interactions between one place and another.' He continues:

> Between the locations there are lines of force which are generated by the relations between the characters. These forces and the subjectivized landscape

which incarnates them are brought into existence in a form which remains more or less definitive for the novel in question by the fateful act of falling in love.[46]

Phyllis Grove's act of falling in love was concurrent with her creation of an 'imaginary topography'[47] which mapped different lines of force from those which connected the few marks seen in the garden and upon the downland before her. She rejected the Wessex landscape in favour of a dream of another land, mediated by her lover. Hardy once described Wessex as a 'partly real, partly dream-country'[48] and for Phyllis Grove, both the landscape before her and landscape she imagines in the Saar have these qualities mixed. Due to circumstances as various as her own sense of duty, currents in the English Channel, Tina's disinclination to pressure her and bad timing, her dream is not realised. But, like Marty South, she is able to point to the graves of Tina and his comrade, and to tend them with a loving devotion. The story ends with the once tended, 'unmarked' graves now 'overgrown with nettles and sunk nearly flat' (66). The 'older villagers' can still recollect the place where the soldiers lie, but once they die and the oral record is gone, Phyllis's story will be lost, and this fact justifies the written record of the tale. Like Hardy's Wessex, and so much of his writing based on oral sources, the story is 'partly real, partly dream', but Hardy was especially interested in this tale to confirm its factual basis with written records as well as the physical marking inscribed upon the landscape. 'The Melancholy Hussar' closes with the actual register of burials, recording the real names and origins of the deserters, and Hardy's research for the tale included old newspaper accounts as well as local oral sources. These facts, and Hardy's close alignment of himself with the narrator, demonstrate that 'The Melancholy Hussar' was an important story for Hardy in his negotiation of the 'real' and 'dream', truth and invention, oral and written.

Before Phyllis takes the decision to elope with Tina and to give substance to the imaginary topography of his native land, she clearly regards him, and their courtship, as unreal. He was 'almost an ideal being to her [. . .] one who had descended she knew not whence, and would disappear she knew not whither; the subject of a fascinating dream – no more' (54). When he proposes, 'this practical step had not been in her mind in relation to such an unrealistic person' (55). Her attitude to their dream-like courtship period is one in which there is no contemplation of her past allegiances or of future consequences. To move from a consideration of space in Hardy, to time, Phyllis's experience of this 'space of time' with Tina, existing apart from past or future, is what Hardy called in other fiction 'a mere interlude'. This is time which is cordoned off from reality, and the forces which govern it are similar to those which, according to Hillis

Miller, govern the 'imaginary topography' mapped onto a real landscape; they are the forces which pattern the act of 'falling in love'. Hardy is clearly preoccupied with this time outside time, and many examples of the 'mere interlude' exist in his works, one being the short story entitled 'A Mere Interlude' in the volume *A Changed Man*. In that story, Baptista Trewthen secretly and impulsively marries an old boyfriend accidentally met while she is forced to wait three days for a ferry to take her home. Cut off from communication with her family (and indeed from the family friend she is travelling to wed), she lives the few days in a dream, unable to consider consequences. When her husband drowns before they catch the ferry to inform her parents of their marriage, her shock and the unreality of this period lead her to keep the marriage secret and to go home to her long-planned wedding as if nothing had happened. Here the 'mere interlude' seems at first to have no consequences, certainly no future, and to exist outside time. Tess Durbeyfield wants the idyllic season of Angel's courtship to go on indefinitely, resisting consideration of the future or the past. Towards the end of the novel, on the run after murdering Alec, she takes shelter with Angel for a few days in an uninhabited manor house. She does not want to leave:

> The gloomy intervening time seemed to sink into chaos, over which the present and prior times closed as if it never had been. Whenever he suggested that they should leave their shelter and go forwards towards Southampton or London she showed a strange unwillingness to move.
> 'Why should we put an end to all that's sweet and lovely!' she deprecated. 'What must come will come.' And, looking through the shutter-chink: 'All is trouble outside there: inside here content.' (*Tess*, 498)

Here both space and time are cordoned off. Tess is happy in a lovers' interlude which keeps at bay past and future suffering. Viviette Constantine, the heroine of Hardy's 1882 novel, *Two on a Tower*, painfully describes her relationship with the younger Swithin St Cleve as 'only an interlude', but her love for him and the regret that their affair may end belie the description of this space of time as inconsequential for the lovers involved (*Two on a Tower*, 108).

The interlude can be as long as a love affair or as brief as a moment's imagining; a shared time, or in the mind of one desiring person. A crucial moment in the fifth story of *Wessex Tales*, 'Fellow-Townsmen', exists as a 'mere interlude' of great intensity. It occurs after Barnet has rushed home with the body of his drowned wife. A doctor has pronounced her dead, but as she lies there he fancies he sees some vestige of life about her, and he turns to medical books and stimulants to attempt once again to resuscitate her. Barnet's wife clearly loathes her husband, and their marriage has been so unhappy that he yearns regretfully for Lucy, the woman he did not marry but still loves. His wife's death would release him, but he still works to save her. Alone with his wife's body, he reaches for restoratives, but in that moment pauses at the view of Lucy's house through the window:

> Pulling up the blind for more light, his eye glanced out of the window. There he saw that red chimney still smoking cheerily, and that roof, and through the roof that somebody. His mechanical movements stopped, his hand remained on the blind-cord, and he seemed to become breathless, as if he had suddenly found himself treading a high rope.
> While he stood a sparrow lighted on the window-sill, saw him, and flew away. Next a man and a dog walked over one of the green hills which bulged above the roofs of the town. But Barnet took no notice. (138)

While the world continues around him, Barnet experiences an interlude outside time in which he is able to imagine himself a free man, able to live his life with the woman he loves. The narrator only conjectures distantly what Barnet may be thinking in that moment; he does not directly make available Barnet's interiority or emotional state, but leaves the reader to enter that space outside time with the protagonist. Barnet is alone, and everyone has been told that his wife has died. 'By merely doing nothing', the narrator states, Barnet could 'deliver' himself from his wretched marriage. Instead he rejoins time and acts vigorously and successfully to save his wife. His movements to resuscitate her are described as 'mechanical', a word also used to describe Phyllis Grove as she walks away from her elopement with Tina and teaches herself to regard her romance with him as a mere interlude: she 'move[d] mechanically onward on what she conceive[d] to be her allotted path' (61). Barnet mechanically but 'calmly' resumes his allotted path of duty, treating the unexpressed thoughts of his momentary interlude as a dream removed from his actual life's path.

Paths and interludes, 'spots of time', 'time-lines': space and time often stand in for each other metaphorically, and do so quite intensely in Hardy. Hillis Miller observes that Henchard's life in *The Mayor of Casterbridge* is seen 'as if his life were a spatial movement that could be graphed as a line',[49] and he considers this conflation: 'To see time as a pattern in space is to see it as determined to follow just the sequence it does follow. Space fatalises.'[50] A retrospective look at the years of one's life as a journey, made up of events whose importance could not be recognised at the time, but which in retrospect assume an inevitability, is to see a pattern in space which was fated to be, which was inescapable. Hillis Miller argues that Hardy's characters can only see this pattern when they are near death, when it is too late to learn from the choices taken, decisions made. By this time they have become detached from their own lives, simply onlookers viewing the pattern that it took. However the 'interlude' may bestow something of this insight before death. The interlude forms a protrusion upon the graphical line of a life. Within the interlude, characters, either imaginatively or actually, experience life and love of great intensity that is seemingly removed from that line of causality, from past acts and future consequences. The end of the interlude, which does not necessarily coincide with the end of desire or love, is often experienced in the fiction as a kind of death, as it is the end of an imagined, illusory or forbidden life within life. This ending or little death brings its own insights, but does not always bring detachment. 'The movement of detachment', argues Hillis Miller, 'is a separation from life in which the character becomes completely changed into an uninvolved witness of all that had once lured him to longing and suffering'.[51] As the narrator, focalising Angel Clare, writes of Tess and Angel's interlude spent in the empty manor house; 'within was affection, union, error forgiven: outside was the inexorable' (*Tess*, 498). Angel at this point is a man changed by experience and suffering, but he is not detached from the world, has not fallen out of love and is not near death. He senses before death that the environment outside the safe haven, beyond the interlude, is inimical to much that is pursued and desired in life. Yet at the close of the novel, with Liza-Lu, Angel resumes his 'allotted path' and rejoins a world of potential desire and suffering: 'As soon as they had strength they arose, joined hands again, and went on' (*Tess*, 508).

Barnet also 'goes on' after his imaginary interlude of freedom, just as he has to do in the second 'interlude' of the story which occurs briefly between the time that he reads the letter announcing his estranged wife's death in London, and half an hour later, the letter from his closest friend asking him to attend his wedding that same morning to Lucy: 'That his few minutes of hope, between the reading of the first and second letters, had carried him to extraordinary heights of rapture was proved by the immensity of his suffering now' (157). The suffering marks him for life, leaving a permanent 'horizontal line' in the 'smooth of his forehead'. And yet Barnet moves on in a 'mechanical condition' towards the church where the wedding is taking place. He resumes once again his 'allotted path', and performs all that is seemly and kind in congratulating his friend and his now-lost love.

Some critics have labelled Barnet a self-destructive character: he acts to save the wife he hates and he does not stop the wedding of the woman he loves.[52] But to act differently would be to diminish the character of this man who is included in Hardy's 'novels of character and environment'. If Barnet were to march purposively down to the church to stop the wedding (as one frustrated critic thinks he should do[53]) he would be robbing his friend of a wife and mother to his children for the second time. It was to help smooth matters in Barnet's marriage that led his friend's wife to accompany Barnet's wife to the shore for an afternoon's jaunt. Downes was bereft when his wife drowned that day, and to take a wife from him again would be to repeat some of that horror and grief. It would be both sensational and cruel.

Instead Barnet enters the vestry to watch them sign their names and forces himself to appear 'calm and quite smiling; it was a creditable triumph over himself, and deserved to be remembered in his native town' (159). They invite him back for a celebration, but he excuses himself, saying 'I'll stand back and see you pass out, and observe the effect of the spectacle upon myself as one of the public' (159). The ensuing moment in the churchyard marks the beginning of Barnet's self-obliteration, after which nothing 'will be remembered of him in his native town' and he will remove himself from the locale to become simply 'one of the public' wherever he is on the globe, unconnected and unknown. He leaves Port-Bredy the next morning after burning his papers and making arrangements for the sale of his home and all his interests in that place:

> By the time the last hour of that, to Barnet, eventful year had chimed, every vestige of him had disappeared from the precincts of his native place, and the name became extinct in the borough of Port-Bredy, after having been a living force therein for more than two hundred years. (161)

Both Hillis Miller and Kristin Brady have noted Barnet's 'pleasantry' at Lucy's wedding that he will stand outside himself to 'observe the effect of the spectacle upon myself as one of the public'. Brady sees it as an example Barnet's 'self-destructive' and 'self-dramatising' tendencies, and of his 'withdrawal from life and emotion'.[54] Hillis Miller writes of the moment as just one example among many in Hardy's writing of 'the movement of detachment', which he describes as 'a separation from life in which the character becomes completely changed into an uninvolved witness of all that had once lured him to longing and suffering.'[55] The last section of the story, however, does not reveal a man who has withdrawn from emotion, or found the relief of detachment, but reintroduces the motif of the marked and inscribed environment and physical body: 'Twenty-one years and six months do not pass without setting a mark even upon durable stone and triple brass; upon humanity such a period works nothing less than a transformation' (162). This reminds us that Barnet still carries the mark, that 'horizontal line' on his brow brought there by the misery and disappointment of hearing of Lucy's marriage, and also introduces an aged Barnet who has 'a deeply-creviced outer corner to each eyelid, and a countenance baked by innumerable suns to the colour of terra-cotta' (163). The fact that Barnet has returned to find Lucy is also evidence that he has not forgotten, has not successfully detached himself. He begins his enquiries concerning former friends and acquaintances in an inn, building up to asking about Lucy, and when he does his body language discovers a man still very painfully involved: an 'attentive observer would have noticed that the paper in the stranger's hand increased its imperceptible tremor to a visible shake'. He regains control by 'closing his lips firmly' and 'dropping his eyes' (165). Barnet makes a last attempt to unite himself with Lucy, but she greets his proposal with blank surprise and a very definite refusal. Shortly after he leaves her house, however, she begins to reconsider, pondering that his pleasant 'urbanity' at her refusal 'was very gentlemanly of him, certainly; it was more than gentlemanly; it was heroic and grand' (172). Lucy gives voice here to the only stated assessment of Barnet's personality in the story, and coming as it does close to the tale's end, it has a ring of authority. Barnet is admirable because he is able to suffer, and to accept an environment and circumstances which are inimical to him, without blaming others, betraying them or causing them to suffer as well.

New Year's Eve of 1885 found Hardy sad and disheartened, as he confessed in his journal. He quotes the stoic Marcus Aurelius, 'This is the chief thing: Be not perturbed, for all things are according to the nature of the universal' (*Life*, 182–3). This is one of Hardy's favourite quotations, and in this moment on New Year's Eve he is not able to be stoical, detached or unperturbed, but nevertheless determines that it would be a good state to try to achieve. Equally, Barnet in 'Fellow-Townsmen' is not detached or uninvolved, but it is 'noble and heroic' for him to attempt to be so, or at least to appear so. Having experienced imaginary interludes which have granted him a vision of an alternative and happier life, he is still able, when circumstances and environment close off that interlude, to take up his 'allotted path'. Rather than a man who exhibits 'a serious imbalance [in] personality', in Kristin Brady's assessment,[56] he is a sensitive and sympathetic character whose 'triumphs over himself' when suffering 'deserved to be remembered in his native town' (159).

The fact that Barnet is remembered by no-one in his native town, except Lucy, is a process of self-obliteration which he had only accelerated; it was already in train while he lived there. His father had sold off his flax manufacture, making an educated 'gentleman' of his son who could live off inherited wealth. The name Barnet is still used as a recommendation or courtesy-name on the gates and warehouses in Port-Bredy, but when he returns twenty-one years later the name is gone and forgotten. Barnet is 'gentlemanly', as Lucy says, but this is part of his problem: first-generation 'gentlemen' and 'ladies' often fail to leave their mark upon the world, to carry on their names in Hardy's writings. Jocelyn Pierston of *The Well-Beloved*, Grace Melbury of *The Woodlanders*, Tess Durbeyfield and Barnet are all examples of those raised to a higher social class by an ambitious parent or through marriage, and they are mostly childless and somehow disappointed or unsuccessful in life. Even Farmer Lodge of 'The Withered Arm,' an active, working man, attempted upward mobility through marrying a young woman of some education and wealth. But his marriage was childless, which in an almost identical echo of Barnet's 'obliteration', 'rendered it likely that he would be the last of a family who had occupied that valley for some two hundred years' (91). Like Barnet, Lodge finally sells off his farms and lands and leaves no vestige of himself in his native place. He moves to Port-Bredy, finalising his self-obliteration in Barnet's native town. Farmer Darton of Hardy's 1884 story, 'Interlopers at the Knap', has inherited substantial farms from his rough and financially wily father, but he himself is more of a gentleman farmer and lacks the drive and energy of his forebears. He is another example of the disappointed expectations of those who have been raised socially above their parents. Darton's ineffectuality exhibits itself in his hesitation in choosing between two women.

While 'The Withered Arm' explored the devastating and occult effects of a female sexual rivalry as it was forced upon two women by social circumstances and male expectations, 'Interlopers at the Knap' focuses upon a situation of potentially fierce rivalry between two women for the hand of Farmer Darton, but this story-line is stopped in its tracks by the absolute refusal of the story's heroine, Sally Hall, to participate in such a competition. Descriptions of female rivalry or its possibility often focus upon women's attire: Gertrude Lodge's new silk dress rustling in the church, or Elizabeth-Jane's acknowledgement to herself that Lucetta 'was a lady much more beautifully dressed than she' (*Mayor*, 153). As Hardy continues in *The Mayor of Casterbridge*: 'Had she been envious she might have hated the woman' (*Mayor*, 154).

A crucial moment in 'Interlopers at the Knap' occurs with the present of a new dress made to Sally by Farmer Darton in anticipation of their approaching wedding. The plot is convoluted, but the tale begins with the farmer and his best man getting lost as they travel in the dark to the remote Hintocks, where Sally and her mother await their arrival (the 'Hintocks' are in fact several hamlets or villages, all with that word as suffix). Supper is laid, the fire blazing, but just before Darton finally finds the Knap, Sally's home, others arrive: Sally's stricken and impoverished brother who has returned destitute from Australia, his wife and two small children (of whom Sally and her mother know nothing). Sally's brother enters the house, confesses his beggarly condition and goes off to bed – in fact to die that night. He informs his mother that his wife and two children are in the stable awaiting his signal that they are welcome. He also tells Sally that when he stopped at a wayside inn there was a parcel for her that he was entrusted to deliver. Finding it was a dress, he gave it to his wife to put on, as she was ashamed of meeting her relatives in such ragged clothing. Sally, especially concerned for the children ('Poor little things!'), goes with her mother to the stable to fetch them into the house and the warm. Upon entering a vignette meets their eyes: Farmer Darton and Helena, Sally's sister-in-law, are standing transfixed by each other, hand in hand. Darton had entered the stable and found Helena, a former love who had refused his hand years before, wearing the dress he expected to see on Sally:

> He seemed to feel that fate had impishly changed his *vis-à-vis* in the lover's jig he was about to foot; that while the gown had been expected to enclose a Sally, a Helena's face looked out from the bodice; that same long-lost hand met his own from the sleeves. (195)

Sally's quick intelligence allows her to take in the situation and recognise it as one of potential rivalry.

Hardy never collected into his four volumes of short stories the early tale, 'Destiny and a Blue Cloak' (1874), but it is a powerful account of a sinister antagonism that one woman feels for her rival. As the rivalry becomes oddly centred in the blue cloak of the title, the story bears some similarities to the preoccupation with the wedding dress in 'Interlopers'. 'Destiny' opens with a young man greeting Agatha Pollin on Weymouth esplanade, believing her to be, by her blue cloak, another woman – in fact her friend Frances from the same village. Oswald Winwood introduces himself because he has heard much of Frances' vaunted beauty. Agatha fails in the first moment to tell Oswald that he has mistaken her identity, because she fears he will excuse himself and go. The mistake continues as they spend a day together. By the time she corrects his misapprehension, on their journey home to her village, he is already smitten by her and tells her, 'It is you I like, and nobody else in the world – not the name'.[57] When their coach stops, Agatha realises that Frances has been travelling with them and has overheard their conversation. A few years later, Oswald is returning from making a name for himself in the Indian Civil Service, and to marry Agatha, but he is too late. Frances has meticulously plotted her revenge, producing circumstances which force her rival to marry an old and sexually avaricious man whom she despises. Frances informs Agatha, married that day and facing the deeply unpleasant prospect of the bridal bed, that Oswald has just arrived from Southampton that morning and that she has told him of Agatha's wedding. She appears before Agatha in the semi-darkness, if not quite the terrifying incubus of 'The Withered Arm' then certainly an evil apparition, almost Gothic in the quiet intensity of her hatred:

> When Agatha was putting on her bonnet in the dusk that evening, for she would not illuminate her ghastly face by a candle, a rustling came against the door. Agatha turned. Her uncle's wife, Frances, was looking into the room, and Agatha could just discern upon her aunt's form the blue cloak which had ruled her destiny. (*Indiscretion*, 33–4)

It is a sinister scene, evocative of that in which the madly jealous Bertha Mason places Jane Eyre's bridal veil on her head before destroying it. Each of these scenes uses articles of women's clothing as the plot device by which one woman can be mistaken for or replaced by another. As a young sea captain says, in 'To Please His Wife', a late Hardy story of female rivalry from *Life's Little Ironies*:

> 'when a man comes home from sea after a long voyage he's as blind as a bat – he can't see who's who in women. They are all alike to him, beautiful creatures, and he takes the first that comes easy . . . '. (146)

Indeed, etiquette books of the day bemoaned a demographic situation in which women had become almost interchangeable with one another: such was the superfluity of women in Britain, that society regarded prospective brides as 'two a penny'.[58] The 1851 census had confirmed that there were more women than men in Britain, a situation affected partly by emigration trends. Victorian society was acutely conscious of what was designated 'The Woman Question' and it is hard to find a periodical from the 1840s on that does not include an article on this question and that of the 'redundant' or 'superfluous' woman. These epithets were used to describe a woman who had failed to find a husband, and who therefore often had to work to support herself. In a society where jobs for middle-class women were few, poorly-paid and limited in scope, most women fervently wished to avoid that genteel and lonely drudgery in favour of a prospect that their culture lauded as their natural role, that of the financially dependent wife and mother. Of course, numerous Victorian novels are plotted around this anxiety over women's marriage prospects in a 'market' that favours men, and the resulting rivalry between women for a partner, but Hardy's writings are peculiarly alert to the damaging effects of this competition. He exhibits the stark passions of jealousy and ambition involved in sexual rivalry, throwing them into sharp relief by focusing the area of their action in small, isolated places. Remote, sparsely populated areas reflect Britain's demographic inequality acutely and intensely. Hence, in *The Woodlanders*, Felice Charmond and Grace Melbury become rivals for Fitzpiers in the very remote Little Hintock, as if he is the only eligible man in the neighbourhood. In terms of class he is the only suitable bachelor around for Felice, and if Grace is to fall in with her father's ambitions, the only one available for her as well.

'Interlopers at the Knap', like *The Woodlanders*, takes place in 'one of the Hintocks (several villages of that name, with a distinctive prefix or affix, lying thereabout)' (179). The story is Hardy's earliest use of this remote setting, and the treatment of sexual competition between women who live in places where suitable men are scarce anticipates the 'struggle for existence' that Hardy would describe two years later when writing *The Woodlanders*: 'the lichen ate the vigour of the stalk, and the ivy slowly strangled to death the promising sapling' (*Woodlanders*, 59). Indeed, most of Hardy's major novels written in the years just before and after he wrote 'Interlopers' concern sexual and romantic rivalry between women: *The Return of the Native* (1878); *The Mayor of Casterbridge* (1886), and *The Woodlanders* (1887). 'Interlopers' is a fascinating commentary upon the rivalry in these novels, and more generally upon the Victorian expectation that women would naturally wish to compete for men.

'Interlopers' opens with Farmer Darton travelling towards the Hintocks down the 'mercilessly' long Long-Ash Lane. His destination is obscure and difficult to find, and the 'neglected lane' 'was sometimes so narrow that the brambles of the hedge, which hung forward like anglers' rods over a stream, scratched their hats and hooked their whiskers as they passed' (179). Travelling to his wedding, Farmer Darton resembles the prince in 'The Sleeping Beauty' cutting back the brambles to awaken the sleeping village and its inhabitants by kissing the princess. Indeed, the wood through which they travel is almost mythically asleep; there is 'a snore from the wood as if Skrymir the Giant were sleeping there' (182). Like Fitzpiers, Darton seems to be the only suitable man in this remote area, and he has found Sally there and come to save her from a lonely single life. The 'Sleeping Beauty' myth is given further play when we are introduced to Sally and her mother, waiting for the arrival of Darton. Time seems to be standing still as the supper waits for his arrival.

When Sally realises that Darton still harbours feelings for her brother's widow, she does not compete for him but, after a few months, actually encourages him to propose to Helena, which he duly does. A couple of years later, Helena having died in childbirth, Darton thinks again of Sally and decides to renew his proposals. Again, the environment and the human marks upon it, create those 'lines of force' that Hillis Miller describes as threaded across real and imaginary contours of the land:

> Darton was not a man to act rapidly, and the working out of his reparative designs might have been delayed for some time. But there came a winter evening precisely like the one which had darkened over that former ride to Hintock, and he asked himself why he should postpone longer, when the very landscape called for a repetition of that attempt. (205)

He journeys down Long-Ash Lane towards the Hintocks once again. The narrator tells us the lane had once been 'a highway to Queen Elizabeth's subjects and the cavalcades of the past [. . .] a national artery' (179). The repeated journeys, made over hundreds of years, encourage Darton to retrace his own journey. He is confident of success, as the seeming timelessness of the landscape gives the impression that nothing will have changed in the Knap and that they will be waiting for him still.

With a comic nod again to fairy tales, and especially to the 'Sleeping Beauty' myth, this does seem at first to be the case. Although the narrator tells us that a crack over the window is a 'trifle wider', and that the servant Rebekah has lost much of her hair, five years later Sally and her mother are still sitting by the fire as if waiting for a prince to restart time. Mrs Hall cannily encourages this view of things by asking Darton shortly after his arrival to 'push up the chimney-crook for me, Mr Darton? the notches hitch' (208). As well as bridging over any awkwardness over the fact that 'he has been a stranger for four [sic] years', Mrs Hall's little request seems, ludicrously, to want to give the impression that she and her daughter have been waiting helplessly for years for the right man to come and do the job.

This little act, together with Mrs Hall's comment to Darton that Sally is 'ungrateful' for refusing him, as she does that night, indicate that the mother has a strong sense of the scarcity of men, and a decided view that single life should be avoided if at all possible. Sally, however, keeps to her quiet and kindly refusal of Darton, in spite of her mother's earlier admonition; 'Wait till you are twenty years older and you will tell a different tale' (189). Darton learns years later (and these are the final words of the tale) 'that Sally, notwithstanding the solicitations her attractions drew down upon her, had refused several offers of marriage, and steadily adhered to her purpose of leading a single life' (214).

Sally Hall is an unconventional heroine in that she refuses to engage in female rivalry for the man she loves, and that when offered the chance again to marry him (although she now no longer loves him), she does not respond to the general panic over the scarcity of men, and the fear of becoming a 'redundant woman'. We never enter her thoughts, and are not offered a psychological explanation for why she refuses marriage: she is simply, as she tells Darton, 'happy enough' as she is (213).

Some indication of why this may be lies in a description of the 'household economy' of the Knap, as Darton travels there to propose a second time: 'That evening Sally was making "pinners" for the milkers, who were now increased by two, for her mother and herself no longer joined in milking the cows themselves' (207). Under Sally's management, the Knap dairy is expanding. This is in contrast to the wealthy Darton, who has inherited rich farmland but who 'had neither advanced nor receded as a capitalist – a stationary result which did not agitate one of his unambitious, unstrategic nature since he had all that he desired' (178). Both Sally's expansion and Darton's stasis are upheld by the narrator as admirable, each in its way; they are both 'happy enough' as they are. Female social mobility conventionally depended upon marriage, and male social mobility upon 'commercial subtlety' (198). Sally and Darton eschew these methods of getting ahead. Sally enjoys a small gain in social mobility through her own hard work and usefulness.

Kristin Brady criticises the character of Sally as 'too rigid' and 'too self-reliant' because she did not marry either Darton or Darton's friend Japheth who proposed to her a few years after Darton's first journey to the Knap. Japheth at least was able to recognise that Sally 'was a woman worth having if ever woman was' (203), as he castigates Darton for replacing her with Helena. But Sally never loved Japheth, and when she did love Darton he seemed not to recognise her uniqueness, taking another woman in her place, another woman in her dress. Brady argues that this sort of love is unimportant in the making of a marriage, next to 'tried friendship' and 'good fellowship', and that, unlike Bathsheba or Elizabeth-Jane, Sally has failed to learn this. Leaving aside the very debatable premise that Hardy forswears the importance of romantic love in marriage, the fact is that Sally no longer respects Darton as she once did: he has mistaken her for another kind of woman – one who is desperate to marry, one who would be driven by sexual rivalry or desire for material gain. To hold that Sally is rigid in her refusal to marry is to become subject to those social and narrative expectations with which Hardy was so impatient; those expectations that the heroine must marry *someone*.

While Sally is 'happy enough' in her life running the business of the dairy, Lizzy Newberry confesses to her 'distracted preacher' of the story's title that the excitement of the smuggling business in which she is engaged means so much to her, that 'if it wasn't for that [. . .] I should not care to live at all' (251). Sally Hall's business makes her independent enough to refuse offers of marriage if she chooses, but Lizzy Newberry is so distracted by the business she loves that she can hardly concentrate when an offer of marriage is being made to her. Stockdale, the young Wesleyan preacher who is in love with her, asks why she cannot give him an answer to his marriage proposal and she replies, 'with embarrassment'; 'Because I am thinking – thinking of something else' (233). Although she has fallen in love with the preacher, her answer to him here is comically removed from the conventional response to a marriage proposal in the literature of the period: it is neither sentimental nor the product of marital scheming. At a time when women were supposed to be thinking of little else but how to get a marriage partner in a country where men were scarce, Lizzy's answer that she is thinking of 'something else' – of smuggling – is quite exhilarating.

Although 'The Distracted Preacher' (1879) appears last in *Wessex Tales*, it was the first story of that volume to be published. Appearing between the publication of *The Return of the Native* (1878) and *The Trumpet Major* (1880) it is imbued with Hardy's grandfather's tales of his smuggling expeditions at the turn of the century, the smuggling tales of James Selby a generation later, and his own childhood memories of a local woman who hid smuggled brandy for sale under her clothes. Again it was James Selby of Broadmayne, Dorset, mentioned in the Preface to *Wessex Tales* as a man employed by Hardy's father for 'over thirty years', who was the chief informant concerning the smuggling of brandy from France in the 1820s and 1830s, the period in which 'The Distracted Preacher' is set. Selby, as discussed earlier, was also an informant for 'The Melancholy Hussar' and gave his last name to the narrator of 'A Tradition of Eighteen Hundred and Four'. As in those two stories, 'The Distracted Preacher' looks out from the Dorset coast to Europe, but in this case the foreign element is not an historical figure, like Napoleon, or a German soldier from Napoleon's wars, but French smugglers in business with their Wessex counterparts. While writing this early story Hardy was engaged in research of the Napoleonic period and local lore from that time for *The Trumpet Major*. In that novel the French and English meet in battle on sea and land, and the ways in which decisions of central government affect men and women in the outlying regions of the nation is played out in the relationships between Bob Loveday the sailor, his brother John the dragoon, and Anne Garland, the local woman they love. 'The Distracted Preacher' tells an alternative story in which the French and English meet at sea and on the beaches, but according to a different configuration by which they are partners and allies against the official central authorities of both France and England. Both the foreign and familiar aspects of storytelling are evident, but the foreign, in this case the French, have become familiar; more so, for example, than the laws and its representatives issuing from London's central government. As Lizzy states 'firmly' to the young preacher, Stockdale:

> 'Why should you side with men who take from country traders what they have honestly bought wi' their own money in France? . . . if a King who is nothing to us sends his people to steal our property, we have a right to steal it back again.' (277)

The story's terrain on the north Wessex coast is 'explored' more meticulously than in any other story of *Wessex Tales*, and this is entirely appropriate for the last story of a volume that is so preoccupied with human marks and traces on the Wessex landscape. The ground is investigated, walked over, by both the central authorities – the outsiders who 'mean nothing' to Lizzy – and by Lizzy herself in her night-time smuggling escapades. Hardy produces three separate lists of places 'tested and examined' by the excise-men to find the brandy tubs, ranging from rainwater butts to cesspools. Stockdale is forced to familiarise himself with the coastal terrain as he secretly follows Lizzy, on her way to 'burn the lugger off' (to light a fire on the cliffs as warning to the smugglers that it is not safe to land):

> On she tripped at a quickening pace till the lane turned into the turnpike-road, which she crossed, and got into the track for Ringsworth. Here she ascended the hill without the least hesitation, passed the lonely hamlet of Holworth, and went down the vale on the other side. (246)

Stockdale sees that 'her intention seemed to be to reach the coast about midnight', and her lack of hesitation as she crosses the rough terrain in the dark, her perfect knowledge of the landscape, force him to acknowledge that smuggling is in her blood. After all, as she tells him later, it was practised by her grandfather and father before her. His mission, both religious and romantic, becomes to get her away from that coast, 'inland' to a 'minister's parlour' far away from what she knows and indeed loves. In this, Stockdale finally succeeds, but only after Lizzy has put up a fight.

Stockdale presents Lizzy with an ultimatum: choose marriage with him, or smuggling. Lizzy struggles with herself, but finally tells him; 'It is too much to ask. My whole life ha' been passed in this way' (281). He leaves her and the village, but returns to renew his proposal two years later, having heard that while he was away a terrible battle had taken place between the excise-men and the smugglers. Lizzy relates the story of the battle to the returned minister and this story within the story is markedly different from its frame. The tone is serious and saddened as she tells of blood-money offered to take the smugglers dead or alive, of her cousin, Owlett, who was shot in the back but survived after they hid him in a barn. She tells Stockdale:

> 'We were hunted down like rats [. . .]. We had a dreadful struggle that last time, when they tried to take him [Owlett]. It is a perfect miracle that he lived through it; and it is a wonder that I was not killed. I was shot in the hand [. . .]. It bled terribly, but I got home without fainting; and it healed after a time.' (285)

As Hardy wrote in the Preface to *Wessex Tales* and in a note added in 1912 to the end of this story, Lizzy's account is based upon actual clashes between smugglers and 'Preventative-men' between 1825 and 1830. The factual basis and Lizzy's suffering lend a graver tone to her tale than that of the romantically comic main story, and this makes it even more difficult to reconcile Lizzy's love of the risk and excitement of smuggling with her departure at the end of the tale as Stockdale's wife to a minister's parlour in a Midland town. Her vehement language ('We were hunted down like rats') and her continuing defiance of the King's men ('We would not let him be took') make her future as the dutiful and obedient minister's wife seem incongruous and rather sad. When producing the Wessex Edition of his writings for Macmillan in 1912 his return to the story prompted Hardy to place a note after this ending, explaining that 'the marriage of Lizzy and the minister was almost *de rigueur* in an English magazine at the time of writing', but that thirty years later he can give his 'preferred' ending, which he claims corresponds more closely to 'true incidents':

> Lizzy did not, in fact, marry the minister, but – much to her credit in the author's opinion – stuck to Jim the smuggler, and emigrated with him after their marriage, an expatrial step rather forced upon him by his adventurous antecedents. They both died in Wisconsin between 1850 and 1860. (287)

So Owlett, who has been shot in the back, and Lizzy, who has been shot in the hand, both emigrate, battle-scarred, from the wild west of England to the Wild West where, quite possibly, they themselves will learn how to handle a gun.

'Wessex', the region comprising the six counties which are the main settings for Hardy's writing, was named so by him after that 'extinct Kingdom' of Anglo-Saxon Britain.[59] The *Wessex Tales* are impressed by vestiges of the Wessex identity as a separate kingdom or country: the remoteness and obscurity of the Hintocks, tracts of downland, Egdon Heath and the wild coastline seem to harbour those who live by alternative conventions and even laws than those 'living under Queen

Victoria'.[60] But one would not want to overemphasise this; Hardy wrote also, as he himself put it, of 'a modern Wessex of railways, the penny post, mowing and reaping machines, union workhouses, lucifer matches, labourers who could read and write, and National school children.'[61] Many of these modern elements appear in *Wessex Tales*, but there remains finally the sentiment engendered by Lizzy Newberry's words about the end of her smuggling business, 'But I had been brought up to that life; and it was second nature to me. However, it is all over now' (285). Lizzy's attitude to smuggling, like that of her grandfather, father and her husband when living, was founded in the conviction that the landscape around her was a region separate from and not bound by the laws of a central government: now that it has become an 'extinct Kingdom' for her, closely monitored by the King's men, she and Owlett emigrate in Hardy's alternative ending, and like so many other characters in *Wessex Tales*, work an obliteration of themselves from their landscape.

In both endings to this last story in the volume, the cousins Lizzy and Owlett, both from generations of smugglers, leave their mark on the landscape. The cellar for the brandy tubs, built under the roots of an apple-tree, was discovered and destroyed by the excise-men; 'But the hole which had in its time held so much contraband merchandise was never completely filled up, either then or afterwards, a depression in the greensward marking the spot to this day' (272). This human mark on the landscape does not carry the pathos of the mark of a grave in 'The Melancholy Hussar', or an execution site in that same story and 'The Withered Arm'; it does not have the old, even ancient history of the paths and by-ways, from Long-Ash Lane to a footpath over downland, 'climbed, foot-swift, foot-sore / By thousands more' ('At Castle Boterel'). Nevertheless it is a place that marks the financial fortunes of the villagers, and their communal efforts and interests.

Lizzy leaves, but she carries the mark of her struggle against central authority with her in the form of the bullet-wound on her hand. In 'The Withered Arm', 'The Three Strangers' and 'The Melancholy Hussar' from *Wessex Tales*, bodies are marked by execution, and these marks are signs on the body of injustice, whether of poverty, neglect or military intransigence. To Lizzy's thinking, the mark on her hand is also a sign of injustice and her people's battle with the 'King's men'. This conflict between the central and the remote, the city and Wessex between which Hardy was continually travelling, is subtly played out in almost all of the stories of *Wessex Tales*. The stories are inscribed by the separateness and independence of that ancient Wessex, the 'extinct Kingdom'.

Notes

1. David Lodge, 'Thomas Hardy as a Cinematic Novelist', quoted in T. R. Wright (ed.), *Thomas Hardy on Screen* (Cambridge: Cambridge University Press, 2005), p. 9. The term 'cinematic' has most often been applied to Hardy's work because, as Wright claims, of 'his self-limitation to what could be seen (from the outside)'. Essays in *Thomas Hardy on Screen* develop this understanding of Hardy's rendering of the visual in verbal description to include (as in Wright's essay especially) narratological elements such as focalisation, the restricted narrator and narrative lacunae.
2. Thomas Hardy, *The Life and Work of Thomas Hardy*, ed. Michael Millgate, p. 33. All subsequent references to this work (abbreviated to *Life*) will be indicated by page number within the text.
3. Hermann Lea, *Thomas Hardy through the Camera's Eye*, p. 38.
4. Ibid., pp. 34 and 38.
5. Thomas Hardy, 'Afterwards', Poem no. 511 in James Gibson (ed.), *The Complete Poems of Thomas Hardy*, p. 553.
6. Ralph Pite, *Hardy's Geography: Wessex and the Regional Novel*, p. 171.
7. *Wessex Tales*, Hardy's first collection of short stories, was published by Macmillan in two volumes on 4 May 1888. This edition included the story 'The Imaginative Woman', which was transferred to *Life's Little Ironies* (1894) upon the publication of the Wessex edition in 1912. At this time two stories originally published in *Life's Little Ironies* were transferred to *Wessex Tales*: 'A Tradition of Eighteen Hundred and Four' and 'The Melancholy Hussar of the German Legion'.
8. Thomas Hardy, Preface to the 1895 edition of *Far from the Madding Crowd* (1874; Wessex Edition, II, 1912). Reprinted in Harold Orel (ed.), *Thomas Hardy's Personal Writings*, p. 9.
9. Ralph Pite, *Hardy's Geography: Wessex and the Regional Novel*, p. 171.
10. Thomas Hardy, 'At Castle Boterel', Poem 292 in James Gibson (ed.), *The Complete Poems of Thomas Hardy*, pp. 351–2.
11. Ibid., pp. 171–2.
12. J. Hillis Miller, *Fiction and Repetition*, p. 118.
13. Ibid., p. 120.
14. George Wotton, *Thomas Hardy: Towards a Materialist Criticism*, esp. pp. 127–31.
15. Penny Boumelha, *Thomas Hardy and Women: Sexual Ideology and Narrative Form*. See for example p. 35, and the discussion of Eustacia Vye, pp. 54–6.
16. Robert Gittings, *Young Thomas Hardy*, pp. 58–61.
17. Quoted in Robert Gittings, *Young Thomas Hardy*, p. 59.
18. K. D. M. Snell, *Annals of the Labouring Poor: Social Change and Agrarian England*, p. 387.
19. Ibid., pp. 386–7.
20. Roger Ebbatson takes an historical approach to the references to arson in his article, ' "The Withered Arm" and History', *Critical Survey* 5:2, 1993, pp. 131–5.
21. Newman Flower, *Just As It Happened*, p. 92.
22. Quoted in Robert Gittings, *Young Thomas Hardy*, p. 58.

23. Thomas Hardy, 'The Dorsetshire Labourer', reprinted in Harold Orel (ed.), *Thomas Hardy's Personal Writings*, p. 168.
24. Quoted in Michael Millgate, *Thomas Hardy: A Biography*, p. 288.
25. In a letter to Rider Haggard of March 1902, included in *Life*, p. 335.
26. Stephen to Hardy, 10 January 1888, in *The Life and Letters of Leslie Stephen*, ed. Frederic William Maitland, pp. 393–4
27. Kristin Brady, *The Short Stories of Thomas Hardy*, p. 21.
28. Ibid., p. 25.
29. Ibid., pp. 12–13.
30. Ibid., p. 16.
31. Quoted in Michael Millgate, *Thomas Hardy: A Biography*, p. 451
32. Walter Benjamin, 'The Storyteller', in *Illuminations*, p. 84.
33. Ibid., p. 85
34. J. Hillis Miller, *Thomas Hardy: Distance and Desire*, p. 1.
35. Kristin Brady, *The Short Stories of Thomas Hardy*, p. 16.
36. Walter Benjamin, 'The Storyteller', in *lluminations*, pp. 91–2.
37. Thomas Hardy, 'Old Furniture', Poem 428 in James Gibson (ed.), *The Complete Poems of Thomas Hardy*, pp. 485–6.
38. Thomas Hardy, 'Afterwards,' Poem 511, ibid., p. 553.
39. Kathryn R. King here quotes from Hardy's 'General Preface to The Novels and Poems, Wessex Edition, I, 1912' as it appears in Harold Orel (ed.), *Thomas Hardy's Personal Writings*, p. 46.
40. Kathryn R. King, 'Hardy's "A Tradition of Eighteen Hundred and Four" and "The Anxiety of Invention"', *Thomas Hardy Journal* (8:2), May 1992, p. 23.
41. Quoted in Martin Ray, *Thomas Hardy: A Textual Study of the Short Stories*, p. 17. originally from R. L. Purdy and Michael Millgate (ed.), *The Collected Letters of Thomas Hardy*, vol. V, p. 326.
42. Walter Benjamin, 'The Storyteller', in *Illuminations*, p. 93.
43. Sophie Gilmartin, *Ancestry and Narrative in Nineteenth-century British Literature*, pp. 222–5.
44. From the 1896 Preface to the Wessex Novels edition of *Life's Little Ironies*, from which 'The Melancholy Hussar' was later transferred to *Wessex Tales*. The 1896 Preface was not reproduced in the 1912 Macmillan Wessex edition.
45. Quoted in Martin Ray, *Thomas Hardy: A Textual Hardy of the Short Stories*, p. 24.
46. J. Hillis Miller, *Thomas Hardy: Distance and Desire*, p. 142.
47. Ibid., p. 142.
48. Thomas Hardy, Preface to the 1895 edition of *Far from the Madding Crowd* (1874; Wessex Edition, 11, 1912). Reprinted in Harold Orel (ed.), *Thomas Hardy's Personal Writings*, p. 9.
49. Ibid. (Orel), p. 198.
50. Ibid., p. 200.
51. J. Hillis Miller, *Thomas Hardy, Distance and Desire*, p. 189.
52. Kristin Brady, *The Short Stories of Thomas Hardy*, pp. 30–1. Brady also notes Ray Morrell's similar response to the character of Barnet.
53. Ray Morrell, *Thomas Hardy: The Will and the Way*, p. 113.
54. Kristin Brady, *The Short Stories of Thomas Hardy*, p. 31.

55. J. Hillis Miller, *Thomas Hardy: Distance and Desire*, p. 189.
56. Kristin Brady, *The Short Stories of Thomas Hardy*, p. 31.
57. Thomas Hardy, 'Destiny and a Blue Cloak', in *An Indiscretion in the Life of an Heiress and Other Tales*, Pamela Dalziel (ed.), (Oxford: Oxford University Press, 1994), p. 14. All other references to this story will be given as *Indiscretion* and the page number in the text.
58. Mrs Humphry, *Manners for Women*, 1897.
59. Thomas Hardy, Preface to the 1874 edition of *Far from the Madding Crowd*, also in Wessex Edition II, 1912. Quoted in Harold Orel (ed.), *Thomas Hardy's Personal Writings*, p. 8.
60. Thomas Hardy, Preface to the 1895 edition of *Far from the Madding Crowd*, reprinted in Harold Orel (ed.), *Thomas Hardy's Personal Writings*.
61. Ibid., p. 9.

Chapter 2

A Group of Noble Dames

On 9 May 1890, Hardy posted off the six stories originally published as *A Group of Noble Dames* to the periodical, the *Graphic*, and immediately set off with Emma for his annual visit to London for 'the season'. It would appear that he had no presentiment to trouble him that the arrival of the stories at the *Graphic* would cause offence and consternation – but Hardy never did seem to be troubled by such presentiments. As Michael Millgate writes, he exhibited a 'curious incapacity to see his work as it might be seen by others, to appreciate its potential impact upon minds and imaginations not precisely attuned to his own.'[1] One can hear the exasperation in the editor William Locker's letter to Hardy from 25 June: he writes that the stories are

> not at all suitable for the more delicate imaginations of young girls. Many fathers are accustomed to read or have read in their family circles the stories in the *Graphic*; and I cannot think that they would approve for this purpose a series of tales almost every one of which turns upon questions of childbirth, and those relations between the sexes over which conventionality is accustomed (wisely or unwisely) to draw a veil.[2]

It is more than likely that those Victorian fathers most decidedly would have wished to draw a veil over the sentiments of Squire Dornell, father to Betty, the 'First Countess of Wessex' in the first tale. The Squire's wife had arranged a marriage for their daughter when she was only thirteen, unbeknown to him and against his wishes. Betty returns from her years of schooling to overhear her father:

> 'I tell 'ee, Sue, 'twas not a marriage at all, in morality, and if I were a woman in such a position, I shouldn't feel it as one. She might, without a sign of sin, love a man of her choice as well now as if she were chained up to no other at all.' (15)

Betty's 'delicate imagination' is revolutionised by this unconventional approach to marriage, which carries the authority of her father. In acting upon it, she comes close to a socially disastrous adultery.

While 'Dame the First: The First Countess of Wessex' was actually not one of the original six sent to the *Graphic*, but was the first of ten stories published in volume form in 1891, it is nevertheless a good example of attitudes and plot-lines that so worried the Directors of the *Graphic*. Another story includes a Lady Chatterley-style visit to the gardener, to suggest he help Hardy's noble dame conceive a child, and another, as Locker wrote to Hardy, 'the hysterical confession by a wife of an imaginary adultery'.[3]

Realising he would have to 'smooth down' the Directors at the *Graphic* (*Life*, 237), Hardy severely bowdlerised the tales, but he returned them almost to their original state when they were published in volume form by Osgood, McIlvaine in 1891. For this volume he added four stories that had also appeared in serial form in other periodicals. The first story of the volume, 'The First Countess of Wessex', and the eighth, 'The Lady Penelope', were written in 1888–89, but the other two, 'The Duchess of Hamptonshire' and 'The Honourable Laura' (the ninth and tenth stories) were early stories published in serial form in 1878 and 1881 respectively. The volume collection of ten stories therefore represents some of Hardy's work in the short-story form over a period of thirteen years from 1878 to 1891.[4]

Many of these stories feature cross-class relationships or marriages and so mirror Hardy's literary career, in which he dealt with this theme in his first novel, unpublished and now lost, 'The Poor Man and the Lady'. This theme is a narrative preoccupation from his earliest works, such as the story 'An Indiscretion in the Life of An Heiress' (uncollected by Hardy into any of his four volumes of stories), and his second novel, *Under the Greenwood Tree*, continuing through to the end of his novel-writing with *Tess of the d'Urbervilles* and *The Well-Beloved*. Viviette, Lady Constantine, the heroine of Hardy's 1882 novel, *Two on a Tower*, is another 'noble dame' who marries below her. However, the complications over whom she has married, and when, can serve as an introduction to some of the confusion and elaborate circumstances that seem to exercise every permutation of marriage, widowhood and adultery in *A Group of Noble Dames*.

Lady Constantine has been abandoned by her estranged noble husband. While he is presumed lost, possibly dead, in Africa, she must wait for his return, however unpleasant that prospect may be. One of the villagers assesses Viviette's uncertain state of limbo: ' "Ah, poor woman!" said granny, "The state she finds herself in – neither maid, wife, nor widow – is not the primest form of life for keeping in good spirits" ' (*Two on a Tower*, 18). When word reaches her from Africa that her husband has been dead for some time, she secretly marries a young man from the village, the poor but educated astronomer Swithin St Cleeve. Several months of happy and hidden married life ensue, but it is eventually revealed to Viviette that her first husband, although well and truly dead, died later than first reported; he was still alive when her second marriage was solemnised, and she is therefore not legally married to Swithin. Hardy writes that 'On first learning of her anomalous position, Lady Constantine had blushed hot' but that she gradually she got used to the idea: 'Women the most delicate get used to strange moral situations. Eve probably regained her normal sweet composure about a week after the Fall' (260).

As with Lady Constantine, so it is with many of Hardy's 'noble dames': they may find themselves in an anomalous position in which there is uncertainty over which phase of womanhood they occupy – maid, wife or widow. Often the circumstances that result in this uncertainty strain credulity, or are even absurdly contrived, as they are in *Two on a Tower*. Hardy is fascinated and troubled by the performative language of the marriage vow. Most of the stories are set well before the introduction of divorce laws, so the marriage contract is irrevocable while entered into by those who are subject to arbitrary, or at least changeable, passions. This combination of the irrevocable vow and mutable passions or circumstances is powerfully incommensurate. But Hardy not only employs this mismatch to fuel the drama of so many of the stories; he creates strained and complicated circumstances which put pressure upon the marriage contract, worrying it to the point of exhaustion or breakage. Seemingly every permutation, every possibility, afforded by the desire to make, keep, break or remember the marriage vow is explored: *A Group of Noble Dames* includes four secret marriages, four runaway wives escaping the legal husband, two widowhoods, two faked widowhoods, one faked legitimacy, one delusional illegitimacy, disguised maternity and paternity and a bigamous marriage. When Hardy published the complete volume of ten stories in 1891 he had been engaged in work on *Tess of the d'Urbervilles*, and was possibly also thinking forward to *Jude the Obscure*; the first novel places the heroine in the no-man's-land of being 'neither wife nor widow' and vulnerable to becoming a mistress, and the second subjects the marriage vow and its duties to such intense scrutiny that Sue sees the ritual as itself enchaining and a curse upon love.

The children of these oddly-plotted unions are the focus especially of three tales: 'Stonehenge', 'Lady Mottisfont' and 'Squire Petrick's Lady'. The frame story's narrator, the 'Sentimental Member', prefaces his tale, 'The Marchioness of Stonehenge', by stating that: 'There was no pathos like the pathos of childhood, when a child found itself in a world where it was not wanted, and could not understand the reason why' (111).

Children are too often the victims of these ill-assorted unions, and in this theme as well Hardy anticipates the child, Little Father Time, in *Jude the Obscure*.

'The First Countess of Wessex', which opens the volume, brings together the themes of victimised childhood and the marriage vow in the one young 'noble dame', Betty Dornell. She appears at the beginning of the story leaning out of a window at night, childishly placing her hands over her eyes in order to shut out the altercation between her parents in the adjoining room. She is only twelve or thirteen years of age, but her parents are fighting over her marriage prospects. Betty is not a neglected abandoned child; she suffers because she is the adored only child and heiress of parents who cannot agree over what they want for her. Betty's mother, Susannah, herself a great heiress, wants Betty to contract an early betrothal to Stephen Reynard, a clever courtier and man of the world who is sixteen years older than she: the Squire is disgusted by this prospect, and insists there shall be no such betrothal. He hopes that when Betty is of age, Phelipson, the young son of his deceased friend, will find favour with her. And so Betty is tossed back and forth between her parents. On the night of the battle that opens the story, the Squire leaves their family seat to go to his own country house. He stays away a few days, but, missing Betty, returns to find that Betty's mother has taken her to London. There, without the authority or knowledge of her husband, she organises and oversees a marriage between her daughter and Stephen Reynard. Although Betty is now married, her husband has promised not to claim her for five years. He pursues his career in foreign courts while Betty is sent to school.

Betty's mother defies her husband's authority, exhibiting an independence of spirit and daring confidence which is most likely gained from her superior wealth. Upon marriage, the Squire left his own estates to live on his wife's vaster and richer lands. This is just one example of how class, wealth and gender cross each other in the power balance between men and women in these stories. It cannot be assumed men will have authority over women: the power balance is frequently reversed and this is a theme returned to repeatedly in the tales.

Writing to the Squire from London in a conciliatory mood, Susannah informs him of the marriage and attempts to excuse her actions. She explains to him that, 'she had felt that no other such fair opportunity for a good marriage with a shrewd courtier and a wise man of the world [. . .] was within the range of probability, owing to the rusticated lives they led at King's-Hintock' (12).

As in *The Woodlanders* and 'Interlopers at the Knap' of *Wessex Tales*, the villages designated by the 'Hintocks' are peculiarly remote, and also in keeping with that novel and story, there seems to be a scarcity of marriageable men. Hence Susannah's urgency: she posts to London with her daughter, to catch Reynard before he leaves for the Continent, and to marry him to her daughter, a 'child just gone thirteen' (11). From etiquette books to *Punch* cartoons to the three-volume novel, it was usually the ambition of the Victorian mother in playing the marriage market that was lampooned or vilified. The narrator describes the 'little figured frock' in which Betty was married as 'pathetic testimony to the small count taken of the happiness of an innocent child in the social strategy of those days' (48). Although the story is set in the previous century, there are shades of the ambitious Victorian mother in Susannah, and Hardy, accustomed now to the social engagements of the London season, would have seen, as Ruskin did, that young ladies were being 'sold' on a nineteenth-century marriage market. Ruskin wrote in 1875:

> as the most beautiful and marvellous maidens were announced for literal sale by auction in Assyria, are not also the souls of our most beautiful and marvellous maidens announced annually for sale by auction in Paris and London, in a spiritual manner, for the spiritual advantage of a position in society?[5]

Susannah's great wealth enables her to move between London and the remote King's-Hintock quite rapidly and with little preparation and planning. She is far more mobile than other characters living in the Hintocks in Hardy's works. Giles Winterbourne and Marty South of *The Woodlanders* and Sally Hall from 'Interlopers at the Knap' move across smaller areas of the Wessex landscape. However, despite Susannah's moneyed mobility, the story itself marks out a specific Wessex space, and the movement is along a few roads and lanes between the Squire's bachelor house and the family seat twenty miles away, and journeys to Bristol. Although Hardy felt that *A Group of Noble Dames* was 'of a somewhat different kind' than his previous writing he made an exception of this first story which he wrote to *Harper's* in 1890, 'comes near it in character'.[6] Indeed, the story is steeped in the landscape of this part of Wessex: Kings-Hintock Court overlooks 'our beautiful Blackmoor or Blakemore Vale' (3) which Hardy is imaginatively exploring at the time of writing the tale for the setting of *Tess*, and Long-Ash Lane reappears more than once in the story, but most importantly as a factor in mildly mocking the enthusiasm of Betty and Phelipson for their lovers' escape on the night that Reynard is expected to come to claim her: 'They left the park by an obscure gate to the east, and presently found themselves in the lonely and solitary length of the old Roman road now called Long-Ash Lane' (39).

Betty and Phelipson's journey along Long-Ash Lane connects them with other lovers who have travelled along that old Roman road in Hardy's fiction. Like those others, they add their own impression to the paths and tracks marked on the landscape by human purpose and desire. The lane is a thoroughfare upon that subjectivised landscape which Hillis Miller has described as

> Form[ing] for the reader an inner space identifying the characters with certain locations in a topography of the mind. The reader is invited to imagine the relations between the characters as tensions between centers of subjective energy reaching across the gaps between those locations.[7]

'Milieu and person, scene and figure' are interpenetrated in Hardy's writing, according to Hillis Miller, and 'lines of force' are created between locations and between the characters associated with those places.[8] As discussed in the previous chapter, characters move between these locations impelled by desire or, as Miller writes, by the 'act of falling in love'. Certain places in Hardy's works however are associated with falling out of love: Rushy-Pond, for example, where Gertrude Lodge pauses to see the scaffold in the distance, is associated with her quest to regain her husband's waning love; it is also the scene of the poem 'At Rushy-Pond' in which the speaker remembers

> I had called a woman to me
> From across this water, ardently –
> And practiced to keep her near;
> Till the last weak love-words had been said,
> And ended was her time . . . .[9]

The scene seems to be the same pool referred to in Hardy's great poem of dying love, 'Neutral Tones' (1867):

> We stood by a pond that winter day,
> And the sun was white, as though chidden of God,
> And a few leaves lay on the starving sod;
> They had fallen from an ash, and were gray.[10]

Similarly, Long-Ash Lane seems to be a weary, discouraging road upon which lovers' wishes are either thwarted or ill-omened, or where there is a falling out of love. 'Interlopers at the Knap' opens with Farmer Darton's journey along the lane, the first of several, which end each time in either digression from love or romantic rejection. The road is 'monotonous', 'tedious and lonely' and, for the weary traveller hoping for its end, 'Long-Ash Lane stretches in front as mercilessly as before' (177). In *The Woodlanders*, Winterbourne drives along what is almost certainly Long-Ash Lane (from the Hintocks to Sherton Abbas) to meet Grace: 'Arrived at the entrance to a long flat lane, which had taken the spirit out of many a pedestrian' (*Woodlanders*, 37), he sees Marty South and offers her a ride. Both her desire for him, and his for Grace to whom he is travelling, are at odds on this journey, and both are fated not to prosper. Although not a story of romantic love, but of the love between a father and son, 'The Grave by the Handpost' (1897) from Hardy's last volume of stories, *A Changed Man*, gives the road as the site for a final act of despair, when the son, is 'found shot through the head by his own hand at the cross-roads in Long-Ash Lane where his father lay buried' (141).[11]

Betty and her lover do not get very far down Long-Ash Lane. Betty is already full of 'misgiving' when she asks to stop at a roadside inn and by the light of the fire, Phelipson sees that Betty is sickening for the smallpox. He promptly takes her back to Kings-Hintock Court where she must climb back up the traditional ladder of lovers' elopement – an abrupt, undignified and almost comic reversal that encourages the reader to dismiss Phelipson as an unworthy and immature lover.

It is Betty's method of contracting smallpox, which, in addition to her experience of and response to the landscape, makes this very much a Wessex tale. Apprised that Reynard is soon coming for her, Betty makes a desperate bid to keep him away. While taking an airing with her mother, she sees a young girl of her own age at a cottage window: 'The girl's face was covered in scales, which glistened in the sun. She was a convalescent from the smallpox – a disease whose prevalence at that period was a terror of which we at present can hardly form a conception' (24). Betty runs into the cottage briefly and returns, very much the rebellious adolescent, to her mother:

> 'There, I have done it now! [. . .] Nanny Priddle is sick of the smallpox, and I saw her at the window, and I went in and kissed her, so that I might take it; and now I shall have it, and *he* won't be able to come near me!' (25)

Martin Ray writes that 'The First Countess of Wessex' 'has the most fully documented historical basis of any of the *Noble Dames*'.[12] Much of the history is gleaned from John Hutchins' venerable *The History and Antiquities of the County of Dorset*, which Hardy owned and to which he frequently referred:

> Squire and Mrs Dornell are based on Thomas Strangways-Horner (1688–1741) and his wife, Susannah (1690–1758), who succeeded to her Strangways family estate at Melbury. Their only child, Elizabeth (born February 1723), married Stephen Fox (1706–1776; hence Reynard) in 1736 when she was just thirteen years of age.[13]

Hardy 'adds' to this history Betty's love for Phelipson, her mother's eventual reluctance for Reynard to claim Betty, and Betty's pregnancy before living with Reynard. Michael Millgate believes that these aspects of the plot are traditional, coming to Hardy from his mother who had grown up in Melbury Osmond, where the Earls of Ilchester ('Wessex' in the story) had their seat. Hardy's mother was also a source for the name of the girl with the smallpox – Nanny Priddle. In the *Early Life*, Hardy's journal entry for 3 September 1887 reads:

> Mother tells me of a woman she knew named Nanny Priddle, who when she married would never be called by her husband's name 'because she was too proud', she said; and to the end of their lives the couple were spoken of as 'Nanny Priddle and John Cogan'. (*Early Life*, 265)[14]

Nanny Priddle is decidedly a minor character in *A Group of Noble Dames*, but that is part of the point. Placing her at a cottage window visited by the heiress Betty acts as Hardy's note to himself that the families of these noble dames were in earlier times 'at plow'[15] on the lands once owned by great historical families like the Paridelles (hence Priddle). This was quite personal family history for Hardy, as his maternal grandmother, Betty Swetman, came from a family of 'small landowners [who] for generations', as Michael Millgate writes, had farmed land 'subsequently absorbed into the Melbury House estates of the Earls of Ilchester'.[16] The 'Nanny Priddle' whom Hardy's mother knew (and who came, as she did, from Melbury Osmond, supposedly the original for 'King's-Hintock') was presumably 'too proud' to have her name changed upon marriage because, one has to suppose, she knew something of her Paridelle history. Although the Paridelles and other families who, like the Durbeyfields, had fallen into decline are well documented in Hutchins, Hardy knew that their humble descendants would have trouble 'keeping their names' (as Nanny Priddle wished to) from oblivion. Hardy takes it upon himself to record many of these names in his works. As he writes *A Group of Noble Dames*, he is thinking of the genealogies of other women who may be working in turnip fields in his time, but who come from a lineage of noble ladies in the centuries before his noble dames existed. Again, he is considering the genealogical ironies of *Tess of the d'Urbervilles*, as is clear in Dairyman Crick's words about local families in that novel:

> 'There's the Billetts and the Drenkhards and the Greys and the St. Quintins and the Hardys and the Goulds, who used to own the lands for miles down this valley; you could buy 'em all up now for an old song a'most. Why, our little Retty Priddle here, you know, is one of the Paridelles – the old family that used to own lots o' the lands out by King's-Hintock now owned by the Earl o' Wessex, afore even he or his was heard of.' (163–4)

(The Drenkhards appear in the second and eighth tales of *A Group of Noble Dames*.)

As mentioned earlier, *A Group of Noble Dames* is, as Hardy felt, 'of a somewhat different kind' to his other works: for one, its main focus is upon heroines of noble blood, or who are wealthy and landed. That Hardy was motivated to write about more humbly-born groups of women and men is abundantly evident in his writing. But there is a particular poignancy to the lists of women's names that he wrote in his journals in the two or three years before publishing *A Group of Noble Dames*. On 1 March 1887, he lists the names of 'four village beauties' recollected from his youth (*Life*, 214–15). And on 13 December 1888, he lists the names of field women remembered from his childhood (they are the 'bevy now underground' from the poem 'At Middle-Field Gate in February'): 'they were Unity Sargent, Susan Chamberlain, Esther Oliver, Emma Shipton, Anna Barrett, Ann West, Elizabeth Hurden, Eliza Trevis . . . ' (*Life*, 233). He can remember their names after thirty or forty years, and groups of women such as these haunt the Wessex landscape of this first story, even though they are only to be glimpsed, like Nanny Priddle, peering out of a cottage window, disfigured by smallpox.

'The First Countess of Wessex' ends with the introduction of the frame narrative, a meeting of the South-Wessex Field and Antiquarian Club. Although 'this Club was of an inclusive and intersocial character', they are not interested in relating stories of humble women. Hardy probably based the structure of *A Group of Noble Dames* on Boccaccio's *Decameron* in which the group of knights and ladies who relate stories to each other are confined to their country villas by a plague raging outside. The South-Wessex Field and Antiquarian Club is confined by a persistent rain that forces cancellation of the various visits to local antiquities and landmarks. They are 'storm-bound', forced to spend the day together in a relatively confined space, and this encourages a breaking-down of social and class barriers. As the volume ends, Hardy will write that each member realises that those barriers will reassert themselves when they meet again outside the Club. The various members are from diverse walks of life, but what draws them together to create a particular atmosphere is that they are all men. The editor of the *Graphic* conceded that the stories were 'very suitable and entirely harmless to the robust minds of a Club smoking room',[17] and in tune with that atmosphere there is the expected nudging insinuation of the Spark and the Crimson Maltster, the cigar-smoking, and various clichéd pronouncements upon the nature of women. However, this frame narrative is quite slim and not obtrusive in structure: when the various narrators interject their comments upon the story they have just heard, their opinions are either so obviously biased or benignly self-satisfied that they are easily dismissed. Instead, we receive stories that, as Hardy admitted in his Preface, 'dramatise' rather than 'eulogise' the lives of these noblewomen. With all the assumptions about women that may reside in the Club smoking room, it is nevertheless a sufficiently robust atmosphere to present women who are just as capable as men of being motivated by powerful sexuality. There is also a frankness in the members' investigation of the power relationships between men and women, and men are by no means always unchallenged figures of authority.

'Barbara of the House of Grebe', for example, reverses the almost hallowed idea (in Victorian culture and in feminist theory) of 'the male gaze'. Here I would differ from Kristin Brady who argues that the Club members see 'these women only as sexual objects'.[18] In 'The Withered Arm' of *Wessex Tales*, Gertrude Lodge worries obsessively about the marks upon and the malformation of her arm because she thinks it makes her husband 'dislike me – no, love me less. Men think so much of personal appearance' (83). But in the second story of *A Group of Noble Dames* it is the humbly-born young husband, Edmond Willowes, who is the object of the gaze. When Barbara and Edmond come to see her parents, Sir John and Lady Grebe, to be forgiven after their elopement, Lady Grebe invites the modest Edmond forward 'in no frigid tone': ' "How handsome he is!" she said to herself. "I don't wonder at Barbara's craze for him" ' (63). Edmond is sent away under the guidance of a tutor to the Continent for over a year so that he may gain the polish and education expected of an heiress's husband, but towards the end of his time there he is burnt in a fire while attempting to save others. News arrives of his accident and disfigurement, and again it is Lady Grebe who 'blurt[s] out' what Barbara and her father thought, but had 'too much delicacy to express':

> 'Sure, 'tis mighty hard for you, poor Barbara, that the one little gift he had to justify your rash choice of him – his wonderful good looks – should be taken away like this, to leave 'ee no excuse at all for your conduct in the world's eyes . . . '. (68)

Barbara and her mother can render the handsome Willowes an object of a sexually appreciative gaze because the power and authority they hold due to their social position and wealth nullifies the more conventional balance of power between men and women.

Martin Ray has commented that the stories in *A Group of Noble Dames* have a 'contrapuntal' relationship with each other. It is true that, as one story gives way to the next, odd lights and refractions fall upon aspects of the previous tale. This is clearly the case between 'The First Countess of Wessex' and 'Barbara of the House of Grebe'. Many of the basic elements of the story are the same: an only child – a daughter and heiress – adored by an ambitious mother and fond father; two lovers – one aristocratic, the other plebeian. The places in the stories where these parallels diverge is telling, and one place where this is apparent is the discovery of who is the object of the gaze in each story. In the first story, at the mean roadside inn off Long-Ash Lane, Betty's plebeian lover is horrified to find that Betty's face is exhibiting the first signs of smallpox: ' "Won't you be a fright in a month or two, poor, poor Betty!" ' he tells her in a panicked giggle and she asks him, ' "Do you hate me because I am going to be ugly and ill?" ' (40). She tells him that no matter how ill or ugly he became, she would never turn from him, but she realises his love is 'only skin-deep'. Upon parting, he 'hung back from imprinting the expected kiss: at which Betty started as if she had received a poignant wound' (41).

Betty's comprehension that she is loved only 'skin-deep' seems to mark her flesh with a 'poignant wound', as physically the smallpox will leave her marked. As in 'The Withered Arm', the woman is an object of the male gaze and begins to think of herself in this way: meeting Reynard, her husband, later that night she exclaims to him, ' "This spotted object is your wife!" ' But when she tells Reynard that her lover has failed to deliver 'the expected kiss', he 'imprint[s] a deliberate kiss full upon her mouth', knowing that he could contract the dreaded disease.

This imprinting, wounding and marking takes an even more dramatic form in 'Barbara of the House of Grebe'. After Barbara's terrified rejection of his mutilated face, Willowes feels that he has been made the object of the gaze, loved only 'skin deep': ' "I was aware that no *human* love could survive such a catastrophe. I confess I thought yours *divine*" ' (76). His objectification seemingly is completed when Barbara, having fled from his wounded body while he was alive, clings erotically to the full-size marble statue of him, which was sculpted from life in Pisa before his accident. The statue arrives long after Edmond's death when Barbara is married to Lord Uplandtowers, and represents Willowes at the height of his attractiveness.

While Barbara's secret adoration of Edmond's statue would seem to be the final phase in her love for him mainly as a sexual object, her visits to the statue present something more complex. She leaves her husband's bed each night to be with her statue. When Uplandtowers spies on her one night, he finds,

> Barbara [. . .] standing with her arms clasped tightly round the neck of her Edmond, and her mouth on his. The shawl which she had thrown round her nightdress had slipped from her shoulders, and her long white robe and

pale face lent her the blanched appearance of a second statue embracing the first. (83)

Barbara was never allowed to go through a sufficient mourning period for her first husband. She was surrounded by parents and family who told her his death was 'for the best' (77). In her contrition for the rejection of her husband, and her sadness over his death she 'longed to build a church-aisle, or erect a monument' (76), but the parson wanted neither. In the absence of a grave or monument, Edmond's statue finally provides her with a site for her mourning. Her response to the statue is not only erotic, but also contrite, and of 'infantine tenderness'. Her 'sobs, and streaming tears, and dishevelled hair' (84), which are usually interpreted as the throes of erotic rapture, may be the signs of a mourning which has been pent up and only now given opportunity for release; the two states are not mutually exclusive.

Most criticism of this story has followed the line of the narrator and indeed of the deeply unpleasant Lord Uplandtowers that Barbara should have loved Edmond as much mutilated as whole. The narrator writes of the statue: 'this perfect being was really the man she had loved, and not that later pitiable figure; in whom tenderness and truth should have seen this image always, but had not done so' (81). After Uplandtowers brutally mutilates the statue to appear as Edmond did after the accident, he justifies the horrific 'lesson' he is about to teach Barbara with, 'A statue should represent a man as he appeared in life, and that's as he appeared' (85). So much of Hardy's writing indicates the impossibility of memorialising the dead as they appeared in life. For Barbara, this statue acts as Edmond's epitaph, his memorial – but as 'The First Countess of Wessex' makes clear, mourning can often produce a version of the departed which is as much about what the living wanted them to be, as what they in fact were. After the Squire's death in that story, his wife Susannah, 'though she had never shown any great affection for him while he lived, awoke suddenly to his many virtues' (44). As Barbara had wanted to do for Edmond, Susannah 'rebuilt the church of King's-Hintock village, and established valuable charities in all the villages of that name' (46). Betty's epitaph for Reynard, years later, in which she 'described him as the best of husbands, fathers, and friends, and called herself his disconsolate widow' (48) has perhaps a better claim to truth, or so the narrator implies: 'people said in after years that she and her husband were very happy' (48). But while this epitaph is closer to how the man appeared in life to his spouse, the language is the standard and clichéd working of so many epitaphs over many centuries. In fact Hardy quotes almost verbatim from his historical source, Stephen Fox's epitaph written by his 'disconsolate widow' upon his death in 1776.[19] Hardy's writing often presents the irony involved in taking epitaphs at their word.

In the brief moments that Barbara becomes reacquainted with her husband in his marked and disfigured guise, both atmosphere and timing are against her being able to accept him. He has been away from her for more than a year of travel and education which has developed his intellect and transformed him as dramatically for the good, as the fire has horrifically changed his outward appearance. She waits alone at midnight in her lonely house, for a man who is almost a stranger to her, and whom physically she will hardly be able to recognise. Her house, Yewsholt Lodge, given to her by her father, 'stood on a slope so solitary, and surrounded by trees so dense, that the birds who inhabited the boughs sang at strange hours, as if they hardly could distinguish night from day' (66). The isolation and gloom of the night scene are almost Gothic and her tense anticipation of her husband finally gives way to a 'sort of panic' after she sees him, as if she were 'in the presence of an apparition' (74). She flees to the greenhouse, but the next morning, by the light of day, her more mature and sensitive nature reasserts itself, and her thoughts are given in free indirect style: 'She should have regarded him as an afflicted being, and not have been this slave to mere eyesight, like a child' (76). But as is so often the case in Hardy's writing, it is too late: her husband has taken her nocturnal panic as a final response and has left the house, leaving her no way of contacting him.

As in the case of another 'noble dame,' Tess of the d'Urbervilles, whom Hardy was creating about this time, the odds are stacked against Barbara. Too much is made of her inability to love her afflicted husband, both by the narrator and much of the critical commentary on this story. As with Tess, the timing is just off – and the loved one cannot be called back so that the right words can be spoken, the wrong impression effaced. Barbara's parents send her husband away before their married life has matured, and Willowes leaves her irrevocably without giving her time to become accustomed to his new face – when it would seem that just a few hours and the light of day would have made all the difference. The frustration and grief caused by human mistiming and misconnection are behind one of the titles Hardy considered for what became *Tess of the d'Urbervilles* – 'Too late, Beloved!' – and this belatedness, as well as precipitancy, are clearly apparent in both these fictions from the early 1890s.

Unlike Willowes, Reynard in 'The First Countess of Wessex' is able to suffer fairly persistent rejection and to wait for a very long time for Betty's mind to change. He is 'a philosopher who saw that the only constant attribute of life is change, he held that, as long as she lives, there is nothing finite in the most impassioned attitude a woman may take up' (43). Combining the sagacity and patience of a man who can give her time, and the impulsiveness and daring of one who will passionately kiss her when she is infectious with smallpox, Reynard is at long last very seductive to his wife. Unfortunately for Barbara, neither her first nor her second husband has Reynard's patience and philosophy. Uplandtowers' 'cure' for his wife's infatuation with Edmond's statue is so cruel that Hardy softened it considerably, and removed much of that character's brutal predilection and sexual motivation in the serial version for the *Graphic*. In the *Graphic*, Uplandtowers lets Barbara's horror at first glimpsing the effaced statue work the cure, but Hardy's preferred version is far more redolent of a savage sexuality: Uplandtowers' method of keeping her in their bed, forcing her to view the candlelit statue for three consecutive nights, is described as 'torture' and a 'scourge'. The old surgeon narrating the story wonders at the subtle complexity of Uplandtowers' cure, and wonders why he 'never thought of the simple stratagem of constant tenderness' (84).

Because Barbara's first husband left her, and her second could never win her love with patience and tenderness, the statue is the only thing upon which she can expend her love, grief and need to be forgiven. Such is her 'intensity of feeling' (84) and her identification with her memorial of Edmond, that, in a reversal of the Pygmalion myth, she kisses the statue and seems to turn to stone herself: 'her long white robe and pale face lent her the blanched appearance of a second statue embracing the first' (83). But her husband's mutilation of Edmond's statue mutilates Barbara: her sensitive, loving and at times dignified nature is transformed to fearful slavishness and a cowed and abject sexual availability to her husband. Whereas Betty, the First Countess of Wessex, produces a numerous family and is able to leave a memorial for Reynard and mourn as his 'disconsolate widow', Barbara dies 'worn out in mind and body' after producing eleven children, only one of which lives to maturity. She is marked physically and mentally by the destruction of her widow's memorial to the husband she loved, and the erasure of her loving memory of him.

Just how crucial the rituals of mourning can be, especially to the widow, informs the plot of the third story in this volume, 'The Marchioness of Stonehenge'. Barbara's mourning was a process of turning her to stone because her memorialisation and love were forbidden and hidden. In 'Stonehenge' two women compete for the title of widow and the right to mourn publicly, but widowhood for these women is not associated, as in 'Barbara of the House of Grebe', with death and infertility, but with a rite of passage that allows life to continue, particularly in the form of the dead man's child.

Lady Caroline is introduced by the narrator, the rural dean, very much as a bored and spoilt aristocrat. 'Satiated' by the flattery and attentions of 'almost all the young noblemen and gentlemen in that part of Wessex', she 'perversely and passionately centred her affection on quite a plain-looking young man of humble birth and no position at all; though it is true that he was gentle and delicate in nature, of good address, and guileless heart' (95). Lady Caroline contracts a secret marriage with this young man and the narrator leaves little doubt that its secrecy is insisted upon so that she can enjoy a sexual relationship with her lover while not losing face socially. Her pursuit of her lover (who remains unnamed throughout the story – a comment upon his plebeian insignificance) is made more piquant for her by mediated desire: her lover is also loved 'fondly' by a young woman of the village, the woodsman's daughter, Milly, to whom he had paid some attentions. An earl's daughter, Lady Caroline is accustomed to getting what she wants, and whether or not the rural dean narrator is influenced by the 'robust' atmosphere of the 'Club smoking-room', it is certainly made clear that Lady Caroline is sexually predatory, enjoying the pursuit of and competition for her lover.

Her husband's 'guileless heart' proves a problem, for, angered one night in her bedchamber when he sees that her passion for him is waning and social regrets setting in, he suffers a heart attack and dies. While at first ('undoubtedly', says the narrator rather vaguely) she felt 'passionate grief' for his death, she is soon addressing the corpse in a manner which is a natural continuation of the argument she was having with him just before he died: ' "Why not have died in your own cottage if you would die! Then nobody would ever have known of our imprudent union, and no syllable would have been breathed of how I mis-mated myself for love of you!" ' (98). While Barbara Grebe of the volume's second story was made fearful by night, solitude, and even by field mice as she hid in the greenhouse, Lady Caroline is completely fearless and uses the cover of night to erase all evidence of her 'imprudent union'. She drags her husband's body out of the house, through the dark woods, to the village, and is cool enough to place his house key in his hand as she arranges his body by his father's cottage door. Like 'Barbara of the House of Grebe' this story plays with a Gothic atmosphere: Uplandtowers' psychological torture of his wife and his terrifying method liken him to the aristocratic and cruel Gothic villain. But in this story Lady Caroline's obsession with social position gives her an unnatural strength, and her callous treatment of her husband's body as she drags it through the woods at night, render her a Gothic, almost ghoulish figure. Later, when she devises a stratagem by which Milly will pose publicly as the dead man's widow, Milly herself registers the ghoulish quality in Lady Caroline's social obsessions: 'I feel as if I had become a corpse's bride', she shivers as Lady Caroline, 'grasping the young girl's hand, slipped [the wedding ring] upon her finger as she stood upon her lover's grave' (103).

The story quickly recovers from the Gothic mode to become much more of a social drama and, at times, social comedy. Milly combines two important rites of passage – wedding and widowhood – in one moment as she accepts Lady Caroline's wedding ring. In the role of a young widow, appearing at church in her weeds, 'she was almost envied her state by the other village-girls of her age' (103). As widow, she is legally independent both of a father and husband, is freer in her movements, and holds a respected and dignified position in her community. Indeed, her indulgence in her sorrow and the rituals of tending his grave are a 'delight' and 'positive luxury' to her, because this is her imaginative courtship, wedding and mourning altogether. As in the previous story, 'Barbara of the House of Grebe', her memorialisation does not represent the man 'as he appeared in life', especially as it is at base a lie, but the narrator implies that the 'gentle-souled' Milly was better able to appreciate the gentle nature of her lover than was the callous and predatory Lady Caroline. When she discovers that she is pregnant, Lady Caroline tries to wrest Milly's ring from her, as well as the respectability of her widowed state, which she now needs for herself. But Milly stands up to her aristocratic rival, and wins. She fights for her right to remember the dead lover, however falsely, as her own and, like Richardson's Pamela, asserts that 'My character is worth as much to me as yours is to you!' (106). She emerges from this battle not only with her reputation intact, but also with Lady Caroline's unwanted child – a gain for Milly as it completes and makes more real her progress from maiden, to wife, to widow, to widow with the child of the man she loved. Through adoption she gains a genealogical connection with her imagined husband.

As in 'The Fiddler of the Reels' (and as in so much of Dickens' work as well), the adoptive bond is often stronger than the biological; this is significant in a volume that is patterned upon 'the pedigrees of our county families, arranged in diagrams on the pages of county histories' (Preface, v). After a childless marriage with the Marquis of Stonehenge, Lady Caroline, having satisfied her social ambitions, years later remembers her humbly-raised son and decides she wants him back. Milly counters that they should give her son the choice of which mother he wants:

' "Flesh and blood's nothing!" said Milly, flashing with as much scorn as a cottager could show to a peeress, which, in this case, was not so little as may be supposed' (109–10).

To Lady Caroline's utter incredulity, Milly's loving and successful son chooses the woman who 'tended me from my birth, watched over me, [and] nursed me when I was ill' (110). The story has an interesting place in *A Group of Noble Dames* as it completely rejects noble pedigree, both its social and biological significance. For all the physical strength of Lady Caroline, a woman capable of dragging a man's body a good distance, it is Milly the woodsman's daughter who has the stronger character.

The concern in *A Group of Noble Dames* with the social and physical aspects of pedigree might raise the issue of eugenics; this term, from the Greek meaning 'well-born', had been used for the first time by Darwin's cousin, Sir Francis Galton, in 1883. Since 1869, when he published *Hereditary Genius: An Inquiry into Its Laws and Consequences*, Galton had produced numerous works that stressed the importance for society of a systematic effort to 'improve the breed of mankind by checking the birth-rate of the unfit and furthering the productivity of the fit'.[20] Angelique Richardson claims that while Hardy did not 'champion eugenics . . . he exploited its language in his fiction'.[21] She cites especially 'Barbara of the House of Grebe' and 'The Marchioness of Stonehenge'. In the former, Uplandtowers' mutilation of Edmond Willowes' statue 'inadvertently touches upon an emergent eugenic aesthetic', according to Richardson, as it follows through Grant Allen's comment upon sexual selection that, 'the ugly for every kind, in its own eyes, must always be (in the main) the deformed, the aberrant, the weakly, the unnatural, the impotent'.[22]

However, while Uplandtowers succeeds in turning his wife in terror from her erotic attraction to Willowes' statue, so strong was her bond with the statue that its mutilation becomes hers; she is psychologically and sexually marred by Uplandtowers' torture. Her obsessive sexual submission to her second husband produces no male heir, and mainly children who die in infancy – hardly a eugenic triumph. The difficulty with Grant Allen's ideas about the beautiful and the ugly, or Galton's fit and unfit, in *A Group of Noble Dames* (let alone outside fiction) is that desire does not seem to cooperate with the eugenic plan and that these categories, despite science, and even in the face of aesthetics and fashion, often remain oddly and arbitrarily in the eye of the beholder. Barbara may be finally repulsed by the disfigured Willowes, but Lady Caroline of 'The Marchioness of Stonehenge' rejects numerous handsome, healthy suitors for 'quite a plain-looking young man' with a weak heart

(95), and Philippa, Lady Mottisfont, of the following (fourth) story, is also 'not very pretty' (116), while her husband – handsome, titled and wealthy – had the choice of the most beautiful women of society. In *The Descent of Man* (1871) Charles Darwin wrote that over time the English aristocracy had gradually become more beautiful, as men of title were able to choose beautiful women in marriage (presumably their titles obviated their need to be beautiful themselves):

> Many persons are convinced, as it appears to me with justice, that our aristocracy, including under this term all wealthy families in which primogeniture has long prevailed, from having chosen during many generations from all classes the more beautiful women as their wives, have become handsomer, according to the European standard, than the middle classes.[23]

Hardy, by the 1890s, was accustomed to and enjoyed the company of attractive aristocratic women, but his diary entry from 15 March 1890 (when he was writing *A Group of Noble Dames*) takes a different perspective from Darwin's on beauty in the best society:

> With E to a crush at the Jeunes to meet the Duke and Duchess of Teck [. . .]. Met Mrs T. and her great eyes in a corner of the rooms, as if washed up by the surging crowd. The most beautiful woman present [. . .]. But these women! If put into rough wrappers in a turnip-field, where would their beauty be? (*Life*, 234–5)

Hardy registers the difficulty of systematising the qualities of ugliness or beauty when these can be improved or disguised by the ephemera of dress, jewellery and a good hairdresser, and when they are, anyway, dependent upon the myriad and arbitrary tastes and predilections of society. The other problem with the eugenically planned love-plot is that the aristocracy hold an ambivalent status. For example, in the sixth story of *Noble Dames*, 'Squire Petrick's Lady', the squire regards the 'blood and breeding' of the nobility as so very desirable that he applauds his late wife for (as he believes) cuckolding him, and leaving him with the child of the Marquis of Christminster: 'his good wife [had], like a skilful gardener, given attention to the art of grafting, and changed the sort' (159). But Angel Clare in *Tess of the d'Urbervilles* tells Tess that 'decrepit families imply decrepit wills, decrepit conduct' and that she is 'the belated seedling of an effete aristocracy!' (297). For Squire Petrick, the aristocracy is both socially and biologically desirable. One could say that the old-fashioned language of 'good breeding', and a knowledge of sexual selection that had long predated Darwin (in gardening, agriculture, and the breeding of livestock and dogs), reassures him of his adulation of the nobility, as much as any eugenic principle. Angel Clare views the aristocracy as inbred rather than well-bred, and therefore weak and degenerate. These opposing views of the qualities of the aristocracy are of course important to these stories, many of which are plotted around the sexual selection of and by aristocratic women.

'The Marchioness of Stonehenge' is a good enough example among a number of others in the volume of the playing out of the confusion over the biological and social qualities of the aristocracy. The unnamed lover and husband to Lady Caroline is 'plain-looking' and has a weak heart, so, eugenically speaking, he would seem to be a poor choice. He is also of humble birth, which makes him either badly bred, or fresh blood, according to which view is taken about 'old families'. Lady Caroline's second husband, the Marquis of Stonehenge, is nobly born but their marriage produces no children. The confusion is also apparent in Angelique Richardson's interesting article, as she gets into a muddle herself: of this third tale she states quite rightly that 'Lady Caroline's second marriage, to the Marquis of Stonehenge, is desirable socially, but not biologically; it bears no fruit', but later in her essay states that the death of her first husband 'luckily' allows her 'to make a new, healthier choice – both biologically and socially'.[24] This contradiction indicates something perhaps of how complex Hardy's approach to pedigree can be, especially as, during the writing of these tales, he is also revising *Tess of the d'Urbervilles* from serial form to book. *Tess* is crossed and re-crossed by the social, biological and historical nuances of genealogy. In 'The Marchioness of Stonehenge', however, Hardy is finally quite clear in his dismissal of eugenics: Lady Caroline's marriage with the Marquis of Stonehenge produces no children while her first marriage to the untitled, unnamed, plain and unhealthy husband bears a son who, if his paternity is disregarded, would seem a eugenic triumph over circumstances. Lady Caroline's biological son is a soldier, the 'finest of the horsemen', 'manly', intelligent and, in her words, 'a noble and worthy son'. But it is the soldier who dismisses the claims of biology by detailing the nurture he has received at the hands of his adoptive mother. He then dismisses Lady Caroline, telling her that Milly '*is* my mother, and I will always be her son!' (110).

A Group of Noble Dames begins with the fortunes of a thirteen-year-old girl whose father considers her a 'child' and whose mother believes her ready for marriage. The local historian who narrates the tale closes by commenting upon 'the small count taken of the happiness of an innocent child in the social strategy of those days' (48). Both the soldier in 'The Marchioness of Stonehenge' and Betty of 'The First Countess of Wessex' are fortunate in that their childish fates are placed with those who love and care for them. The soldier knows it could have been otherwise and tells Lady Caroline that she cared little for him when he was 'weak and helpless' and abandoned by her. The fourth, fifth and sixth stories of *A Group of Noble Dames* are concerned in varying degrees with very small children; those who are 'weak and helpless' and are vulnerable to the vagaries of the adults who have control over them. Stephen Reynard of 'The First Countess of Wessex' gave some thought to the welfare of the child Betty by at least giving her time to grow up, and when she became a young woman he again gave her time to experiment and mature. The acceptance of mutability, that desire can change – and suddenly – is a sign of Reynard's sagacity, and he does not judge harshly Betty or women more generally for a certain degree of erratic eroticism or romantic feeling before marriage (or in his case before his marriage is consummated). However the sudden changes of desire in 'Lady Mottisfont', 'Lady Icenway' and 'Squire Petrick's Lady' are less forgivable as they are directed towards very young and vulnerable children.

Of the three, 'Lady Mottisfont' depicts the most vividly the cruel abandonment of a child. The abandonment is especially disturbing because most of the story, prior to the child Dorothy's dismissal from her family, has been told by the Sentimental Member in such a way that the reader has become sympathetically invested in Philippa's yearning for her adopted child. Philippa, the rather plain but gentle daughter of a mere squire, is sought in marriage by the handsome, urbane Sir Ashley Mottisfont. In proposing, he asks her if she would take an interest in 'a little waif I found one day in a patch of wild oats' (116). Philippa agrees and after going to visit the baby, just eighteen months old, regularly at the cottage where she is cared for, asks Sir Ashley if she can bring her home to 'bring her up carefully, just as if she were her own' (117). Scenes of idyllic family harmony and happiness follow and Kristin Brady has noted the 'tongue-in-cheek' tone which surfaces: 'the farcical quality in these scenes of idyllic happiness causes the reader, especially in the light of the story's subsequent incidents, to question the initial appraisal of Philippa as an entirely "innocent" and "amiable" woman'.[25] Certainly the Sentimental Member is revelling in sentimentality, to the point of risking an ironic inflection, and Kristin Brady is quite right that 'narrative tone' is crucial to an understanding of the story. However, it is problematic for the reader to need the light shed 'by the story's subsequent incidents', to have to read retrospectively, for a proper evaluation of the characters who drive this tale.

As the narrative unfolds in a first-time reading, the possibility of ironic narrative tone is there, but it is more than balanced by the narrator's convincing description of Philippa's fear and disbelief that Dorothy may be taken from her and her believable and painful conversations with her husband on the subject. Dorothy's biological mother, a beautiful and wealthy Italian Contessa, moves into the neighbouring mansion and begins delicate negotiations to win the heart of, and then to adopt the child. These negotiations are drawn out over time, and over the main length of the story. In the *Graphic* version, Sir Ashley is 'callous, proud, drives his first wife to suicide and discards his child'.[26] He has the aristocratic ruthlessness of an Uplandtowers. In the volume version, he is kind-hearted, but oddly unable to engage with his wife's suffering. His siding with the Contessa and his hints that the child should go to her, are extended over the story and are finally as damaging as Uplandtowers' slow torture of his wife.

Much of the pain in the tale is delivered through dialogue (there is much conversation in this tale). One of the most tortured scenes is between Philippa and 'her' little girl, now almost four years of age: when Philippa asks her, 'where would you rather live, always; with me, or with her?' the child, fascinated by the beautiful and charismatic Contessa, 'looked troubled. "I am sorry, mamma; I don't mean to be unkind; but I would rather live with her; I mean, if I might without trouble, and you did not mind, and it could be just the same to us all, you know" ' (126–7). It is a scene that betrays all the hallowed conventions of the relationships between mother and child as usually presented in the Victorian period. But Dorothy is only four, and as Squire Dornell said of his thirteen-year-old girl when she agreed to wed, ' "What she said means nothing [. . .]. The words be not the child's" ' (11). Dorothy childishly cannot see why it could not 'be just the same to us all'. Philippa however takes her at her word and 'this self-sacrificing woman', as the narrator says, gives the child up to the Contessa.

Her loss of Dorothy drives her to attempted suicide, from which her husband saves her. Months of grieving ensue, 'but he often caught her in tears over some doll, shoe, or ribbon of Dorothy's' (128); he takes her north 'for a change of air and scene'. After the extended torment, the suicide attempt and the mourning for her child, the story suddenly changes and begins to come to a conclusion quite abruptly. Sir Ashley and Philippa return from the north to eventually hear from the Contessa that she is about to remarry and, to escape the discovery that Dorothy is her illegitimate child, she wants to return her to them. But to Sir Ashley's, and the reader's, incredulity, Philippa no longer wants Dorothy. She has recently given birth to a son and coolly tells her husband that the child made her choice and that she 'should prefer not to have the responsibility of Dorothy again' (131). Dorothy is returned, permanently, to the 'kind cottage-woman' who raised her as an infant.

The Contessa and Philippa both callously abandon the child, but while this may fly in the face of the most sacred of Victorian sentiments – the belief in the maternal instinct, the mother's bond with her child – Hardy's writing does include mothers who are quite capable of neglect and abandonment of their children. Arabella in *Jude the Obscure* sends her son from Australia to become Jude and Sue's responsibility, and Car'line, in 'The Fiddler of the Reels' from *Life's Little Ironies*, literally loses no sleep over her little daughter's abduction by her former lover, while the child's adoptive father lies awake full of terrible imaginings. While Hardy often depicted loving mothers, it may be that in these cases he was reacting to the sentimentality and near-worship of motherhood. The distanced and rather tired response to this near-cult is evident in his poem, 'The New Toy'. In the first stanza

> She cannot leave it alone,
> The new toy;
> She pats it, smooths it, rights it, to show it's her own,
> As the other train-passengers muse on its temper and tone,
> Till she draws from it cries of annoy: – [27]

Both Philippa and the Italian Contessa 'greedily' compete for the possession of Dorothy and then in turn discard her. But the possibility that she was simply 'a new toy' is much easier to entertain in the case of the Contessa than of Philippa; the tale is focalised mainly through the latter and the reader has closely followed her suffering and grief for the greater part of the tale. Indeed William Wallace, reviewing *A Group of Noble Dames* in the *Academy* in 1891, felt that Philippa's 'double passion for and rejection of Dorothy [. . .] involve too large a draft on one's credibility'.[28] The comparison earlier between Uplandtowers and Sir Ashley Mottisfont may give a clue to Philippa's mysterious abandonment of Dorothy: Uplandtowers' deliberate and slow torture of Barbara and the extended torment which the mild but intransigent Sir Ashley inflicts upon Philippa through his hints and negotiations over Dorothy's removal, are perhaps similar in that both women become changed in nature after the 'scourge' has been inflicted. Barbara's character is as damaged and disfigured as her first husband's statue, and equally Philippa seems damaged as well. Formerly meek and maternal, she effectively and authoritatively silences her husband when he offers the return of Dorothy. Both women have been 'broken in', subjected to the vagaries of their aristocratic husbands. Their personalities are not continuous with that presented in the earlier part of their stories, and through suffering they finally reject that which they loved.

At the close of the previous story, 'The Marchioness of Stonehenge', Lady Caroline's 'weak and helpless' baby has grown to man's estate, and the strength and independence that enable him to escape the vagaries of aristocratic patronage come as a relief. It is also a relief at the end of 'Lady Mottisfont' that Dorothy, the narrator tells us, having been raised a cottager, has grown up 'robust if not handsome' and

> married, I believe, a respectable road contractor – the same, if I mistake not, who repaired and improved the old highway running from Wintoncester south-westerly through the New Forest – and in the heart of this worthy man of business the poor girl found the nest which had been denied her by her own flesh and blood of higher degree. (132)

As an illegitimate child, there will be no trace of Dorothy on the Mottisfont pedigree. The aristocracy in these stories tend to erase the traces of those who are undesirable by birth or marriage, just as the sturdy Lady Caroline, 'to avoid leaving traces in the road, carried [her dead husband] bodily across the gravel' (100). So it is comforting to learn that Dorothy marries a 'worthy man' who understands those traces and marks on the Wessex landscape, discussed in the previous chapter. The 'old highway' has been travelled for centuries by humble and aristocratic: it is a mark on the landscape that traces their history, whether or not they have noble, written pedigrees. It does not deny connection, but marks the interconnected histories of Wessex inhabitants. The man who can 'repair and improve' that ancient road without destroying it, is a fitting husband for Dorothy, who must accept her painful childhood past while repairing and improving upon it.

In his 1894 story 'The Fiddler of the Reels' Car'line and her illegitimate child come to Ned Hipcroft in London travelling on an open-carred 'excursion train': the little girl is very cold and 'lets out' to Ned, 'in tones that told of a bursting heart. "And my totties be cold, an' I shan't have no bread an' butter no more!"' (176). Dorothy's feet are also cold when she returns to the cottage-woman: 'for a long time, her little feet, which had been accustomed to carpets and oak floors, suffered from the cold of the stone flags' (132). Hardy often closely observes children's needs and ailments, and also the various responses to them on the part of adults. Ned Hipcroft responds by catching the little girl in his arms and eventually lovingly raising her as his own. Sir Ashley Mottisfont buys Dorothy 'thick shoes with nails in them' but fails to raise her as his own, or even to properly educate her. Just as Hardy depicts various aspects and degrees of maternal affection, so he does for the paternal. In these tales of aristocratic women, fathers are not relegated to the stereotypical role of the patriarch who either hinders or consents to a marriage, but are often strongly bound and motivated by love for their children.

Anderling, the foreign lover 'of Dutch extraction' of the fifth story, 'Lady Icenway', feels a 'deep and growing tenderness' for the child he has never seen (143). After revealing to Maria Heymere, as they sail to his estates in Dutch Guiana, that he has married her bigamously, she furiously commands him to allow her to return to England, to announce herself as his widow, and makes him promise that he 'would never molest her, or come again to that part of the world during the whole course of his life' (140). He loads her with jewels and bonds and parts from her; she returns to her uncle's Wessex estate to play the part of a respectable widow, and to raise their infant son.

Anderling later returns to England to announce that his first wife has died and that he can now legitimise their union and their child's birth, but typically in Hardy's works, time is out of joint, and Maria has recently married Lord Icenway. Imperious as ever, she informs him that her husband is 'an excellent man of ancient family and possessions, who had given her a title, in which she much rejoiced' (142). That title has made Maria even more haughty, and in 'the play of slave and queen' (from Hardy's poem 'She Charged Me') that fuels their courtship, this makes Anderling more enamoured, more subservient. Again, she makes him swear to leave, 'never [to] trouble her more' (143).

However, just as in the Sentimental Member's tale the tears of the Contessa and Sir Ashley do not finally mean much, so the oaths of service and obedience that Anderling swears do not hold him (as neither did the marriage vow). He returns yet again, having lost his considerable wealth 'by reckless gambling in the Continental hells to which you banished me' (144). Desperate to see his child, he takes the job of undergardener on the Icenway estate, filling this post for two years: 'Owing to his loneliness, all the fervour of which he was capable – and that was much – flowed now in the channel of parental and marital love – for a child who did not know him, and a woman who had ceased to love him' (145–6).

Anderling uses a high-flown language of courtly love in his relationship with Maria, and she enjoys the power that she holds acting the part of queen to his slave. Through his self-abasement she is able to feel like royalty even before she gains Icenway's title. Kristin Brady, in her excellent reading of this tale, states that 'the romantic counterpoises of humility and haughtiness may be useful during courtship but are absurdly inappropriate in marital and parental love.'[29] Courtly love is dependent upon the loved object being distant (but as Anderling makes clear by his returns to Maria, still in view), and the poetry of courtly love emphasises the eyes that gaze at the beloved who is on a pedestal, unattainable and untouchable. How very inappropriate this is for the needs of children which Hardy meticulously and fondly observes as including cold feet, chilblains, the need for bread and butter and (as Elfride does to the noble Luxellian children in *A Pair of Blue Eyes*) the wiping of runny noses. Clearly, Anderling wants to be able to raise his child, to perform these mundane but essential functions that require closeness and touch rather than a yearning distance, but Maria forbids him to make himself known to his child and only once does she begrudgingly allow him to kiss his boy as he sleeps. These scenes emphasise the father's love (the mother's is hardly in evidence) and help to make Anderling a pitiable, sympathetic figure, the 'unfortunate father', as the narrator terms him.

Brady argues that Anderling's love for his son 'is described in terms more genuine – uncluttered by the language of any convention – than is his adulation for Maria [. . .]. This most stylised of lovers is, as a father, pathetically true to life.'[30] Anderling's love for his child is moving and convincing, but part of his punishment for his culpable bigamous passion for Maria may be that even his love for his child is tainted with the ideal, distanced love which is a feature of the courtly tradition: his little boy asks of his mother, 'That gardener's eyes are so sad! Why does he look so sadly at me?' (147). The yearning gaze of the courtly lover is, for Anderling, very painfully inappropriate to his regard of the child, and while it is not his fault or choice that he cannot be closer or more familiar, it may be that Anderling knows no other way to love but from a distance. He certainly put distance between himself and his wayward first wife, loved Maria at a courtly remove, and at first loved an ideal of his boy, for whom 'he felt a deep and growing tenderness, though he had never once seen the child' (143). His paternal love is not allowed to move much beyond this ideal, and finally, Anderling takes a certain pleasure in his idealising distance: 'a pleasure to himself which, though mournful, was soothing, his lady never forgiving him, or allowing him to be anything more than "the gardener" to her child' (147).

In his relationship with Maria, Anderling could be said to live out his fantasy of self-abasement: since their bigamous marriage the social distance between them has greatly increased. They were a fairly equal match in gentility, and he the superior in wealth. She gains a title and he becomes her gardener: he must serve her every whim. As the language of their encounter reveals, this service becomes quite exciting for Anderling, and possibly for Maria, when she comes to him in his cottage under the garden wall to ask him to make love to her. Lord Icenway has castigated her for not producing a 'lineal successor', and realising that she will not conceive by her lord, she devises a plan to graft Anderling's stock onto the Icenway line and asks for his help. Unfortunately, Anderling is dying and cannot do his lady this last service. However, the deathbed scene, although one of falsehood and illusion, is a pleasurable end for Anderling. She tells him:

> 'You must get well – you must! *There's a reason.* I have been hard with you hitherto – I know it. I will not be so again.'
>
> The sick and dying man – for he was dying indeed – took her hand and pressed it to his lips. 'Too late, my darling, too late!' he murmured.
>
> 'But you *must not* die! O, you must not!' she said. And on an impulse she bent down and whispered some words to him, blushing as she had blushed in her maiden days.
>
> He replied by a faint wan smile. 'Ah – why did you not say so sooner? Time was . . . but that's past!' he said. 'I must die!' (147–8)

Maria returns to the blushes of her maiden days, when she was as yet unattained. She both apologises to him and offers herself, but it is, in keeping with Hardy's fascination with belatedness, 'too late'. The *petit mort* almost coincides with the deathbed scene, but there is an exquisite, and comically depicted, pleasure for Anderling in Maria's belatedness and the impossibility of their union. He dies the consummate courtly lover, enjoying even in death the deferral of desire.

Upon Anderling's death, Lady Icenway allows herself to enjoy a secret widowhood: 'Her harshness seemed to come trebly home to her then, and she remorsefully exclaimed against herself in secret and alone. Her one desire now was to erect some tribute to his memory without its being recognised as her handiwork' (148). She has a title, and can rest secure that any threat to her child's legitimacy or her good name is removed by her 'first husband's' death. She can turn her mind to other matters, and since Lord Icenway prefers 'cocking and ratting' to courtly love, and spends 'the greater part of his time in field-sports and agriculture', she has 'ample opportunity' to do so (143). Her thoughts turn to Anderling and the remote and surprising possibility arises for the reader that she may have loved him, despite her entirely selfish manipulation of him. Some evidence of this is given earlier in the tale: the narrator states that she 'had no conscious love left for him' (144) which could imply that it is buried within her, unrecognisable to herself. When she meets him years after their parting, she refuses his marriage proposal, but the narrator states:

> She had dismissed her poor Anderling peremptorily enough; yet she would often after this look in the face of the child of her so-called widowhood, to discover what and how many traits of his father were to be seen in his lineaments. (143)

Certainly Anderling never gains a glimpse of these feelings, and Maria's formidable desire for noble title and position mean that she keeps them well under control. But the satisfaction of worldly ambition and widowhood create a freedom to indulge in the softer emotions. Lady Caroline in 'The Marchioness of Stonehenge' turns to the memory of her abandoned son and wishes to fill her widowhood with an indulgence in a belated maternal affection. Lady Icenway indulges in the 'luxury' of mourning (as it was in Milly's faked widowhood in 'Stonehenge') and a belated and socially safe 'love affair' with the memory of her dead first husband. Like 'Barbara of the House of Grebe', she mourns the first while married to the second, and like Barbara, feels the need to erect a monument of some kind in memory of the beloved. Hardy's poem, 'Her Secret', concerns a woman's secret mourning and makes an interesting comparison with the forms of grieving, epitaph-writing and monumentalising in *A Group of Noble Dames*:

> That love's dull smart distressed my heart
>   He shrewdly learnt to see,
> But that I was in love with a dead man
>   Never suspected he.
>
> He searched for the trace of a pictured face,
>   He watched each missive come,
> And a sheet that seemed like a love-line
>   Wrought his look lurid and numb.
>
> He dogged my feet to the city street,
>   He followed me to the sea,
> But not to the nigh, still churchyard
>   Did he dream of following me![31]

Women's secrets hold an important place in Hardy's writing: they may be what happens in a 'mere interlude', that space outside time when events seem to have no consequences, or may be a secret like Fancy Day's remembered love passages at the close of *Under the Greenwood Tree*, Barbara's 'little harmless secrets' from Uplandtowers, or Tess's very harmful secret revealed to Angel Clare. They disclose an interiority, which is usually an opening into a depth of character. Interestingly, Lady Icenway's secret mourning and epitaph for Anderling reveal almost no depth of character. Her mourning is similar in plot but very different in tone from the poem 'Her Secret'. She has a stained-glass window made for the church, inscribed 'Erected in his memory by his grieving widow', and when her husband views it and says he cannot ever remember seeing the gardener's wife, Lady Icenway replies 'blandly': 'But she didn't live with him, and was never seen visiting him, because there were differences between them; which, as is usually the case, makes her all the more sorry now' (148). Maria's self-cynicism here, revealed in that phrase, 'as is usually the case', discovers at her own expense that she is fully aware that she could not appreciate Anderling while he lived, and that her mourning is an indulgence she can easily afford because it costs her nothing – not her reputation, title or wealth. She enjoys the illusion of depth that is granted by secrets and mourning rituals, but finally the story returns her to the surface: her real regret is simply that she went to Anderling too late to conceive a 'lineal successor' that would silence the complaints of her morose and grumpy husband.

Three of the four stories that precede 'Lady Icenway' in *A Group of Noble Dames* depict women who to greater or lesser degrees falsely memorialise the dead lover or husband: they fail to remember him 'as he appeared in life'. So it is conceivably refreshing that Lady Icenway cynically recognises the illusory foundation to her sensibility, and this provides some perspective on the illusion – or in fact, delusion – under which Squire Petrick's lady suffers in the following story of that title.

Annetta, the wife of Squire Petrick, dies shortly after giving birth to their first child, a son. On her deathbed she confesses to her husband that the child is not his. Although she does not own to who the father is, her christening of the child by the name Rupert, and her husband's recollection after her death that she had been infatuated with Rupert, the young Marquis of Christminster, seemingly discover to him the facts of the case. After vowing to her to give the child every care, the Squire rushes to the sickbed of his grandfather to have the child excluded from the will, and the 'newly-born infant, who had been the centre of so many hopes, was cut off, and scorned as none of the elect' (155). Such is Squire Petrick's initial response to an intruder in the family pedigree.

But Annetta had suffered under a delusion, as the Squire learns several years later from the doctor who had treated his wife's family. Her love for the Marquis 'had been a delicate ideal dream – no more' (162), and the child is in fact legitimate. Having imparted this news, the doctor questions him, 'You look down in the mouth?' and Petrick sighs, 'A bit unmanned. 'Tis unexpected-like'. As Kristin Brady has remarked, 'Preposterously, Timothy is "unmanned" by the fact that he has not been cuckolded.'[32] His disappointment stems from the reversal of what had really become his own 'delicate ideal dream', that his son and heir (he had the child reinstated by changing the dates on the will) was of noble blood, on one side at least. He had begun to admire his wife's 'lofty taste':

> and the justification for his weakness in loving the child – the justification that he had longed for – was afforded now in the knowledge that the boy was by nature, if not by name, a representative of one of the noblest houses in England. (158)

Annetta, the noble dame of this story, exists only to make a false confession and to die in childbirth by page three. Timothy Petrick is not noble and not a 'dame', but the story shows him making efforts to reach both attainments. The years before he learns that his child's nobility was his late wife's delusion constitute a long gestation of the child to which he wants to give birth: he reads the histories of the Dukes of Southwesterland, his son's supposed forebears, 'studie[s] prints of portraits of the family' and closely begins 'to examine young Rupert's face for those historic curves and shades that the painters Vandyke and Lely had perpetuated on canvas' (160).

In an ironic trope upon Wordsworth's 'the child is father to the man', Timothy thanks God 'he was not as other meanly descended fathers' (159). His wife's 'grafting' had, like that of a 'skilful gardener', connected his pedigree with a noble line, and Timothy wants to forget his own parentage by in a sense fathering himself with his child's attributes and noble history. In this, Timothy repeats a delusion suffered by many parents down the generations, and certainly down the Petrick pedigree, that one's personal ambitions and aspirations can be satisfied by one's children, that it is possible to be reborn through one's child. When the child fails to provide the parent with the desired vicarious life, the damaging effects to both parent and child are made clear at the close of the tale. Timothy's manner 'grew colder and colder' towards the son whom he had loved even before he suspected his aristocratic lineage. Such is his disgust with his own pedigree that he almost disowns Rupert because he is his own. Rupert's bewilderment at his father's disappointment that he is not like the Marquis ends the story: 'Why? How can you expect it father, when I'm not related to him?' (163). His confusion over his father's coldness and their drastically changed relationship recalls the thoughts of the frame story's Sentimental Member upon rejected children and the terrible 'pathos' of the child who is made to feel unwanted, but cannot 'understand the reason why' (111).

'An Imaginative Woman', Hardy's 1893 story from *Life's Little Ironies*, revisits, in an inverted form, this genealogical rejection of the child. Ella Marchmill, like Annetta Petrick, also has a 'delicate ideal dream', in her case of a poet she never met but with whom she nevertheless became infatuated. At the time of her youngest child's conception and during her pregnancy, Ella grasps whatever private moments she has to gaze secretly upon the photograph of the literary Robert Trewe. In keeping with early modern, and later, beliefs concerning 'monstrous births' by which the experiences of the pregnant woman could be imprinted upon the foetus (Hardy calls it 'Nature's trick') Ella's child bears a marked likeness to the poet. Ella dies in childbirth, leaving a boy who is doubly orphaned when at two years of age the suspecting father traces the lineaments of the poet in his face. 'Get away, you poor little brat! You are nothing to me!' are the last lines of the story, and this harsh ending emphasises for both stories how the 'delicate ideal dream[s]' envisioned by either father or mother are anything but delicate or ideal when so cruelly visited upon the children (*Life's Little Ironies*, 31).

'Squire Petrick's Lady' is the only story in *A Group of Noble Dames* in which the central characters are neither noble nor female. And yet Timothy Petrick's grandfather, of the same name, may very well have bought up the estates of many of the noble ladies in this volume. The narrator claims that Petrick Senior's 'skill in gaining possession of fair estates by granting sums of money on their title-deeds has seldom if ever been equalled in our part of England' (153). This canny lawyer's business acumen means that he has been able to gain the vast estates of impecunious and debt-ridden aristocrats; while they are on the wane, the formerly humble Petrick pedigree is preparing its own place in the history books. Indeed, Hardy based the story upon the account of a Peter Walter in Hutchins' *History and Antiquities of the County of Dorset*, who used the knowledge gained as steward to a number of aristocratic estates to acquire 'an immense fortune' in the first half of the eighteenth century.[33] While the story is set in the middle of the eighteenth century, Petrick's social mobility would have been especially resonant in the Victorian period when those made wealthy through trade were both buying up the landed estates of the nobility and gaining peerages as well. Samuel Smiles, in his best-selling self-help manual of 1859 sees this phenomenon as very encouraging for the working man:

> No class is ever long stationary. The mighty fall and the humble are exalted [. . .]. Many barons of proud names and titles have perished, like the sloth, upon the family tree, after eating up all the leaves; while others have been overtaken by adversities which they have been unable to retrieve, and sunk at last into poverty and obscurity [. . .]. The great bulk of our peerage is comparatively modern, so far as titles go; but it is not the less noble that it had been recruited to so large an extent from the ranks of honourable industry.[34]

While old Petrick had been extremely industrious, by the time the story begins, there is little need for the third generation, his grandsons, to be so. They will inherit the vast estates, and the Petrick ambition turns itself to the work of gaining a title. Young Timothy Petrick's brother duly marries an Honourable Harriet, but Timothy has married Annetta, whose family were of the professional classes, for love. Until her deathbed confession, 'he had never found reason to regret his choice' (154). Like Darton and Barnet in *Wessex Tales*, or Grace Melbury in *The Woodlanders*, whose fathers have been industrious before and for them, Timothy does not fit the mould of his forebears; 'he was the single one of the Petricks then living whose heart had ever been greatly moved by sentiments which did not run in the groove of ambition' (154). It is then all the more striking and devastating to him when these ambitions are oddly awakened by his wife's supposed adultery with a nobleman. His desire for an aristocratic child is borne not so much of social ambition (he can never publicly admit his boy's illegitimacy), as from an ideal dream of the innate intelligence, beauty and power of the nobility.

Annetta's ideal dream about the Marquis of Christminster was the sort of delusion that had been carried along the female line; the doctor tells Timothy that her grandmother and mother also suffered from these false dreams. But carried along the Petrick male line is this equally false dream of the inherent superiority of the nobility. Something of the character of the story's narrator, the Crimson Maltster, comes through in the fact that he tells a story warning of a blind love for aristocracy, in the midst of a gathering devoted to a group of noble dames. A retired businessman 'of comfortable means', the Maltster is touching and intelligent in his comprehension of social hierarchy and how it will leave him out in the cold. In the conclusion of *A Group of Noble Dames*, the frame story explains that the Maltster understands the various social, moral and intellectual reasons why, after they leave the evening fireside in the museum, 'on the following market-day his friends the President, the Rural Dean, and the bookworm would pass him in the street, if they met him, with the barest nod of civility' (235). The pointedness of his ignoble tale, and his rueful understanding of social divisions among the South-Wessex Field and Antiquarian Club, endow him with a dignity and credence among the various narrators.

'Anna, Lady Baxby' is also based in part upon a family history in Hutchins' *History and Antiquities of the County of Dorset* and is set in the period of the English Civil War. It concerns a noble lord's besieging of a castle inhabited by a beautiful noblewoman, and would therefore seem ripe for the language of courtly romance. However just as courtly love was inappropriate to the marital and parental exchanges of 'Lady Icenway', it is not pertinent to this seventh story of the volume (and the last of the six original stories published in the *Graphic*) as it concerns itself mainly with the love between a brother and sister.

Lord Baxby, the husband of the tale's heroine, is away raising forces for the King when Parliament forces gather around Sherton Castle. They are led by Anna's noble brother William, who 'was set to reduce the home of his own sister, whom he had tenderly loved during her maidenhood, and whom he loved now, in spite of the estrangement which had resulted from hostilities with her husband's family' (168).

Anna daringly rides out from the castle to parley with him and he entreats her to desert her husband and his politics: 'Anna – abide with me! [. . .] Blood is thicker than water, and what is there in common between you and your husband now?' (169). He attempts to persuade her that fraternal love is stronger and has more 'in common' than marital love. But Anna replies in words which Hardy takes almost verbatim from Hutchins, as said by the original 'Anna', Lady Anne Russell of Sherborne Castle: if he destroys the castle, 'then you will find the bones of your sister buried in the ruins you cause!' (169). Anna's reply indicates that her castle is her home, and that she will stay by her husband's side.

Later that night however, after a political quarrel with her husband, and brooding over her brother's exhaustion and also his love for her, she becomes instead a 'home-hating truant' and prepares to leave the castle in disguise to join her brother. The plot is orchestrated to follow the typical patterns of an elopement or adulterous absconding, and this serves to highlight how it is different; although a very strong and tender love exists between William and Anne, certainly stronger than anything we see between her and her prosaically 'well-fed' and 'well-dressed' husband, it completely lacks any sexual element. This sexuality is the point upon which the story turns, and which turns Anna from Parliamentarian to loyal subject, when, as the Colonel narrates, 'like a mangle, [she] would start on a sudden in a contrary course, and end where she began' (164). Escaping from the castle to her brother that night, disguised in her husband's clothes, she is mistaken by a young woman for Lord Baxby. The girl has an assignation with Anna's husband on the terrace, and her plaintive tones suggest to Anna deep feeling; ' "How the wench loves him" she said to herself'. Mediated desire and sexual jealousy stop her escape in its tracks and she returns to her husband's bed, 'as firmly rooted in Royalist principles as any man in the Castle' (173). Anna's sudden revulsion is comic of course, but it is in keeping with Hardy's portrayal of how sexual jealousy and mediated desire can defy principle, reason, and in this case a love of brother and sister which it is implied has more 'in common' at its base and is deeper than marital love. Eustacia Vye in *The Return of the Native* and Joanna of the 1891 story 'To Please His Wife', collected in *Life's Little Ironies*, are just two examples among many of women who are almost helplessly manipulated, the puppets of sexual jealousy and desire.

In stories based upon 'the pedigrees of county families' (Preface, v), the sexual jealousy such as Anna experiences is crucial because it returns her to her place – her castle and her husband. Her brother's plea to 'abide with me!' would, from the genealogical perspective, lead her nowhere;

brothers and sisters hang off the branches of the family tree alongside each other but do not combine. In the genealogical narrative, sibling love is less important because it does not carry the line forward; in literary narratives as well it usually does not carry the plot forward, and is, if not completely ignored, then certainly downplayed in comparison with courtly, marital, paternal and maternal love, all of which are portrayed in *A Group of Noble Dames*. With the 'diagrams' of county family pedigrees before him Hardy 'finds himself unconsciously filling into the framework the motives, passions, and personal qualities' (Preface, v) which would seem to explain the relationships and juxtapositions upon the pedigree. He fills in the framework, or in the case of sibling love, the lacunae in genealogical and literary narratives, and shows that it is as subject to personal vagaries, chance and changeability as all the other relationships that can be read in a pedigree or story.

With the last three very short stories of *A Group of Noble Dames*, much of the 'contrapuntal' effect between the tales falls away. As these stories unfold, each does not comment upon its predecessor to the degree that the other tales did; there is less of the anticipation and retrospect that helps the reader to think of the volume as a coherent whole. 'Lady Penelope' was written for *Longman's Magazine* and published in 1890, the year before the volume edition of *A Group of Noble Dames*, but the last two stories are among the earliest Hardy wrote. 'The Duchess of Hamptonshire' was his second short story, published after the uncollected 'Destiny and a Blue Cloak' of 1874 (uncollected in Hardy's lifetime and discussed in Chapter 1), and 'The Honourable Laura' had first been published in *Harper's* in 1881.[35] Their separate publication history does explain why they seem at first slightly anomalous – although it is also the case that the first story 'The First Countess of Wessex', which was not one of the original six *Graphic* stories, set the tone for the ensuing tales in the volume. Nevertheless, a closer investigation does discover a number of those preoccupations by which Hardy was exercised in every genre he attempted.

Hardy had recourse yet again to Hutchins' *History and Antiquities of the County of Dorset*, and to the Trenchard family pedigree, for the tale of 'Lady Penelope', based on Lady Penelope Darcy who married her first husband in the early years of the seventeenth century.[36] The Hutchins' account tells that

> She was courted by her three husbands at one time; but quarrels arising between them, she artfully put an end to them, by threatening the first aggressor with her perpetual displeasure; and humorously told them, that if they would be quiet and have patience she would have them all in their turns, which at last actually happened.[37]

Hardy kept very close to the Hutchins and this history had an obvious appeal for him: Hardy is fascinated of course by genealogical repetitions,[38] but he is also clearly both disturbed and inspired by other forms of repetition, series and 'rows'. As Tess says of her place in a genealogical series:

> 'Because what's the use of learning that I am one of a long row only – finding out that there is set down in some old book somebody just like me, and to know that I shall only act her part; making me sad, that's all.' (162)

Avice Caro, in the 1892 serial version of Hardy's novel *The Well-Beloved*, expresses her anxiety to her lover Jocelyn Pierston as she watches him burn letters from past loves; 'I am – only one – in a long, long row!'[39] Whether these successions are made up of 'begetters, dwindling backward each past each' (from Hardy's poem 'The Pedigree'), or a series of lovers or a succession of husbands, as in the case of 'Lady Penelope', those who make up a number in the series experience a fear or sadness that they are insignificant, will simply repeat what came before, or be forgotten. Certainly Lady Penelope's second husband remembers her jest that she will marry all three suitors in turn; for her to fulfil this prophecy, he knows she must be widowed twice, and he is next in line to go. Since he suspects what the narrator verifies, that Lady Penelope has secretly harboured feelings for the man who will become her third husband when she was married to the first two, this does not improve his mood, or allay his fear that he will be a forgotten number in the series.

Lady Penelope's secret (and suppressed) love for the third husband, Sir William Hervy, again returns to Hardy's interest in women's secrets. Fear of losing reputation or being deemed indelicate results in so many circumstances and emotions that women may not express, and this results in secrets which lead to miscommunication, 'letters under the carpet', belatedness and so many of the ironies and 'satires of circumstance' (the title of his 1914 volume of poems) which pervade Hardy's fiction and poetry.

'Delicacy of feeling' finally destroys Lady Penelope's third happy marriage. Unfounded rumours begin to circulate that she murdered her second husband, and Sir William's fine feeling prevents him mentioning them to her. Instead, his doubts canker his marriage and he leaves her without explanation. When the rumours finally reach her, she is unable to write to her husband to claim her innocence as it is 'too degrading'. He reaches her on her deathbed, but it is too late to save her. These miscommunications are frustrating possibly to the reader, but they are reminiscent of all that is left unsaid in many of Hardy's fictional relationships, the most famous example being of the missed letters between Tess and Angel Clare. *A Group of Noble Dames* is replete with epitaphs and the question of whether or not they can represent the dead, as Uplandtowers says, 'as [they] appeared in life'. In 'Lady Penelope', rumours almost become her epitaph: the 'vile scandal' unjustly misrepresents her in life, and actually disfigures and 'withers' her, just as injustice in 'The Withered Arm' disfigures Gertrude Lodge. Lady Penelope is described thus: 'dwindled thin in the face, and the veins in her temples could all be distinctly traced. An inner fire seemed to be withering her away' (186).

It is perhaps odd that the 'Quiet Gentleman' of the frame story who deems Lady Penelope's sad end a 'chastisement' for her youthful jest, is given the role of narrator for the next tale; he has judged that lady harshly, but extends a rather unconventional sympathy to the 'Duchess of Hamptonshire' of the penultimate story, in her desperate flight from her marriage. In love with her austere father's curate, Alwyn Hill, but forced into marriage with a duke, Emmeline writes to Hill, begging him to meet her. The fact that within 'a group of noble dames' she is known only as 'Emmeline' throughout the tale serves to emphasise her vulnerability and lack of class ambition. She has heard that Hill is emigrating to America and she begs to come with him. Her life is intolerable because her jealous and sinister husband, like Lord Uplandtowers, 'adopts plans I dare not describe for terrifying me into a weak state, so that I may own to anything!' (196). Alwyn refuses to take her, much as he loves her, and emigrates to become a professor of rhetoric in Boston. But her pleading with him that night before he leaves proves her to have the true force of argument on her side and a claim to the most persuasive rhetoric in the tale, a rhetoric that is used to justify her desire to break the marriage vow. In fact her questioning of the vow is reminiscent of Squire Dornell's desire that his own daughter should break hers in the very first tale of *A Group of Noble Dames*; first and last, Hardy worries the binding words of the marriage ritual to the point of breakage. When Alwyn tells her it would be a sin, she so argues with him that he can only lamely respond that, 'It would look wrong, at any rate, in this case' (197). She raises the image of a God who watches her suffering as a play or 'sport'; 'Can it be that God holds me in derision?' (197). This story from his early career (an early version of this tale was published in 1878) asks similar questions to those in his later writing, as in *Tess of the d'Urbervilles*, the final paragraph of which states that 'the President of the Immortals, in Aeschylean phrase, had ended his sport with Tess' (*Tess*, 508). To Emmeline's questioning of her God, Alwyn can only respond with the weakness of social considerations: 'Emmy, you are the Duchess of Hamptonshire, the Duke of Hamptonshire's wife; you must not go with me!' (197). For all Alwyn Hill's religion, philosophy and education, he resorts to the most conventional position in refusing to take Emmeline with him. He has been compared to Angel Clare in this,[40] but unlike Angel he never sees his love again and cannot forgive and be forgiven. Instead, Hill unwittingly buries Emmeline at sea, not knowing her true identity. She had followed him 'like a poor pet animal that will not be driven back' (205) and with no money, died of a fever as an unknown and unnamed steerage passenger. Loss of name and death is the usual fate of the runaway wife in most Victorian narratives, most often because this fate is deemed a chastisement for breaking the marriage vow. In this tale, the sympathy for the tormented woman causes the blame to be laid at the feet of the priggish lover who would not help her break that vow.

Further strain is placed upon the sanctity of marriage by the sheer muddle and sensationalism of the last tale of the volume (but with the previous story, 'The Duchess of Hamptonshire', among the earliest that Hardy wrote). 'The Honourable Laura' had first been published ten years before under the title 'Benighted Travellers'. This contemporary tale, the only one in the volume with a modern setting, is relegated to the 'Spark' within the frame story of *A Group of Noble Dames*. This small-town sophisticate, rather past his prime, relishes the *frisson* imparted by the tale of a runaway bride, but finally returns to the safety of a moral outcome for the heroine. Laura has indeed got herself into a muddle as she runs away with her singing teacher Smittozzi, while followed by her father and her cousin James, to whom she is secretly married. All come together in a half-deserted hotel on the 'north coast of Lower Wessex': the disgusted father leaves, James challenges Smittozzi to a duel and Smittozzi takes the opportunity to push James off a high cliff.

This is a Christmas story, first published in *Harper's Weekly* on 10 and 17 December 1881, and certain conventions of either the supernatural or the sensational can be expected: the story even begins, surely parodically, with the sentence, 'It was a cold and gloomy Christmas Eve' (209). But for all the excitement of the story's first half, the rest of the tale is slow and very muted. After she escapes, this time from the suspected murderer Smittozzi, she returns to the hotel to find her husband who, incredibly, has not died. She nurses him sedulously and after a time asks him, 'if I [. . .] always attend to your smallest want, and never think of anything but devotion to you, will you – try to like me a little?' (229). But James is, perhaps understandably, still cross after being pushed from a cliff, so he tells her, 'I don't like you' and leaves for twelve years. There is no further 'plot' as such – nothing actually happens to bring the tale to a conclusion. Laura lives, as her servants say, like a nun in her mansion, remorseful and devoted to the memory of a husband for whom, before his accident, she held a strong dislike. But James returns, and impressed with her good behaviour, stays. His return transforms the 'forlorn home of Laura Northbrook' to a mansion blazing with hearth fires; 'the apathy of a dozen years came at length to an end' (234). By the following Christmas, 'a son had been added to the dwindled line of the Northbrook family' (235). It is an entirely conventional happy ending and as unbelievable as James' surviving a fall from a north Cornish cliff. Hardy's story from *Wessex Tales*, 'Interlopers at the Knap', had gently ridiculed Farmer Darton by inviting comparisons with the fairy-tale revival of the household in 'The Sleeping Beauty'. But James does just this in 'The Honourable Laura' and there is no narratorial sneer or note of incredulity to be heard. We are to believe apparently that James's nasty temper and Laura's child-like tantrums and immorality have simply metamorphosed through time; no explanation or interiority is given.

One could argue that there is some plausibility in ending *A Group of Noble Dames* with its weakest story: Hardy has it narrated by the 'Spark' and the response of his listeners is 'some surprise', for nobody had 'credited him with a taste for tale-telling' (235). He is not a natural storyteller, the tale is weak and the evening is petering out. It is time for them to go home. Hardy probably realised that the stories were of uneven quality. He wrote a letter to Lord Lytton, describing the volume as 'a rather frivolous piece of work, which I took in hand in a sort of desperation during a fit of low spirits'.[41] Still, it is hardly likely that he purposely placed the most flawed story last, and it is also the case of course that some contemporary critical opinion did not see the story in such a way: William Wallace wrote in *The Academy* that 'the first and last stories are the most enjoyable of the series', and that 'Mr Hardy's power of plot construction was indeed never more strikingly illustrated than in "The Honourable Laura" '.[42] It would seem that Hardy wanted to make the stories up to ten for the volume version, probably in imitation of Boccaccio's *Decameron*, and as 'The Honourable Laura' is the only story of contemporary date, it brings the time up to the present for the members of the South-Wessex Field and Antiquarian Club as they go their separate ways at the close of the evening. They are described as 'benighted', echoing the original title of the last story, and which, in their case, could mean that they have been overtaken by night, but could also refer to their moral or intellectual darkness. They are, as the frame narrator tells us, of an 'inclusive and intersocial character' (49) and their views and judgements upon a group of women are as mixed and sometimes at odds as they are.

Comments from the narrators that declare, for example, that Barbara of the House of Grebe should 'by law' have longed to hear the footsteps of her husband, or that Lady Penelope's fate was a 'chastisement' from God, reveal the occasional demonstration of benighted and conventional morality. However, *A Group of Noble Dames* is fascinating because, in addition to its few powerful tales, it is a volume that continually revises itself as it proceeds. And this is nowhere more apparent than in its treatment of gender, and the intersection of gender and class. A volume ostensibly about noble women, it nevertheless presents loving fathers as well as mothers; plebeian adoptive mothers and fathers; neglectful mothers; wives and widows; devoted, courtly husbands as well as the cruel; imperious and submissive wives; and a fraternal love which almost wins over the marital. Such myriad facets and permutations of human relationships produce an overall effect that is tolerant; enlightened rather that benighted.

Notes

1. Michael Millgate, *Thomas Hardy: A Biography*, p. 316.
2. Letter from William Locker to Thomas Hardy, 25 June 1890. Quoted in Martin Ray, *Thomas Hardy: A Textual Study of the Short Stories*, p. 72.
3. Ibid., p. 73.
4. Martin Ray, *Thomas Hardy: A Textual Study of the Short Stories*, p. 69.
5. John Ruskin, *Notes on Some Principal Pictures Exhibited in the Rooms of the Royal Academy, 1875*, p. 20.
6. Thomas Hardy to *Harper's*, 7 March 1890. Quoted in Richard Little Purdy, *Thomas Hardy: A Bibliographical Study*, p. 66.
7. J. Hillis Miller, *Thomas Hardy: Distance and Desire*, p. 140.
8. Ibid., pp. 136 and 142.
9. Thomas Hardy, 'At Rushy-Pond', Poem No. 680 in James Gibson (ed.), *The Complete Poems of Thomas Hardy*, pp. 713–14.
10. Thomas Hardy, 'Neutral Tones', Poem No. 9, ibid., p. 12.
11. Long-Ash Lane seems also to be the road described in Hardy's poem of exhaustion and discouragement, 'The Weary Walker'.
12. Martin Ray, *Thomas Hardy: A Textual History of the Short Stories*, p. 79.
13. Ibid., p. 79.
14. In this case I quote from *The Early Life of Thomas Hardy* by Florence Emily Hardy rather than Michael Millgate's edited version of this work which establishes the text as Hardy would have left it at his death. Florence Hardy had added in the full names of Nanny Priddle and John Cogan; they were left out in Hardy's version.
15. Michael Millgate, *Thomas Hardy: A Biography*, p. 12.
16. Ibid., pp. 9 and 12.
17. Quoted in Martin Ray, *Thomas Hardy: A Textual Study of the Short Stories*, p. 72.

18. Kristin Brady, *The Short Stories of Thomas Hardy*, p. 90.
19. Martin Ray, *Thomas Hardy: A Textual Study of the Short Stories*, pp. 79–80.
20. Entry for 'Sir Francis Galton' in *Encyclopaedia Britannica*, 11th edn, pp. 427–8.
21. Angelique Richardson, ' "How I mismated myself for love of you!": The Biologization of Romance in Hardy's *A Group of Noble Dames*', *Thomas Hardy Journal* (14:2), May 1998, p. 71.
22. Grant Allen, 'Aesthetic Evolution in Man', *Mind*, V (1880) p. 448. Quoted ibid., p. 68.
23. Charles Darwin, *The Descent of Man, and Selection in Relation to Sex*, p. 654.
24. Angelique Richardson, ' "How I mismated myself for love of you!": The Biologization of Romance in Hardy's *A Group of Noble Dames*', pp. 67 and 71.
25. Kristin Brady, *The Short Stories of Thomas Hardy*, p. 68.
26. Martin Ray, *Thomas Hardy: A Textual Study of the Short Stories*, p. 107.
27. Thomas Hardy, 'The New Toy', Poem No. 710 in James Gibson (ed.), *The Complete Poems of Thomas Hardy*, pp. 739–40.
28. William Wallace, 'New Novels', review of *A Group of Noble Dames*, in *Academy*, 40 (1891), p. 153.
29. Kristin Brady, *The Short Stories of Thomas Hardy*, p. 72.
30. Ibid., p. 72.
31. Thomas Hardy, 'Her Secret', Poem No. 302 in James Gibson (ed.), *The Complete Poems of Thomas Hardy*, p. 365.
32. Kristin Brady, *The Short Stories of Thomas Hardy*, p. 75.
33. Martin Ray, *Thomas Hardy: A Textual Study of the Short Stories*, p. 122.
34. Samuel Smiles, *Self-Help*, pp. 210–11.
35. Martin Ray, *Thomas Hardy: A Textual Study of the Short Stories*, pp. 141, 146, 157.
36. Ibid., p. 141.
37. John Hutchins, *The History and Antiquities of the County of Dorset*, III, 329. Quoted in Martin Ray, *Thomas Hardy: A Textual Study of the Short Stories*, p. 142.
38. See especially Chapters 6 and 7 of Sophie Gilmartin, *Ancestry and Narrative in Nineteenth-century British Literature*, which deal specifically with Hardy and genealogy. See also Sophie Gilmartin, 'Geology, Genealogy and Church Restoration in Hardy's Writing', Chapter 2 in Phillip Mallett (ed.), *The Achievement of Thomas Hardy*; Tess O'Toole, *Genealogy and Fiction in Hardy*; J. Hillis Miller, *Fiction and Repetition*.
39. Hardy made significant changes to this novel from the 1892 serial version to the 1897 volume publication. This quotation from the 1892 serial version is included in the appendices to the edition published by Macmillan: Thomas Hardy, *The Well-Beloved*, ed. Edward Mendelson, intro. J. Hillis Miller, p. 206. Avice is right in more ways than she can know, as Jocelyn will go on to love three generations of 'Avice Caro'; herself, her daughter and granddaughter, seeing in all three just one woman, the incarnation of his 'well-beloved'.
40. Kristin Brady, *The Short Stories of Thomas Hardy*, p. 82.

41. Hardy to Lord Lytton, 15 July 1891, in *The Collected Letters of Thomas Hardy*, ed. R. L. Purdy and Michael Millgate, I, 239.
42. William Wallace, 'New Novels', review of *A Group of Noble Dames*, in *The Academy*, 40 (1891), p. 153.

Chapter 3

Life's Little Ironies

The stories that comprise *Life's Little Ironies* (1894) date from the same five-year period: one from 1888, five from 1891 and two from 1893. Given this relatively concentrated time-span, it is unsurprising that the volume as a whole shows a marked consistency in choice of theme and situation. The earliest story, 'A Tragedy of Two Ambitions' (1888), revolves around the inability of two brothers to transcend their humble origins in order to pursue a successful career in the Church – like many of Hardy's characters, they live in the shadow of previous generations, whose influence they resent – while the final story, 'An Imaginative Woman' (1893), concerns, among other things, the inability of a mother to discharge her responsibilities towards her children.

The volume as a whole seems obsessed with the failure of nineteenth-century men and women to negotiate a creative and meaningful relationship with both the past and the future, and this general concern with legacies is given a sharp focus by Hardy's anxiety at this time over the status of his own literary legacy, both in its interpretation of the past and in its susceptibility to misinterpretation in the future. The complex pressures that are brought to bear on Hardy's idea of the present as a condition that has no identity of its own, and no monopoly on the reception and transmission of historical meaning, are introduced in 'A Tragedy of Two Ambitions' through the strange condition of historical suspense that the two brothers are forced to operate in: 'His ambitions were, in truth, passionate, yet controlled; so that the germs of many more plans than ever blossomed to maturity had place in him; and forward visions were kept purposely in twilight, to avoid distraction' (80). In one way, Joshua Halborough thinks of little besides his own future, while in other way, it is precisely any form of thinking forward in time that he must continually suppress. When the social embarrassment of having a miller for a father is finally removed, by their deliberate failure to act quickly enough to save him from drowning, Joshua and Cornelius can look forward to a much smoother fulfilment of their ambitions. But in the event, they make little headway in their careers, remain haunted by their sin of omission, contemplate suicide, and even regret the lives they might have had as millers themselves. The story ends by noting the odd circumstance of their father's walking stick, relinquished in his final moment, having taken root and flourished. Joshua had pushed it into the mud to hinder identification of the body, but it has sprung into life more effectively than any of the brothers' schemes for advancement:

> From the sedge rose a straight little silver-poplar, and it was the leaves of this sapling which caused the flicker of whiteness.
> 'His walking-stick has grown!' Joshua added. 'It was a rough one – cut from the hedge, I remember.'
> At every puff of wind the tree turned white, till they could not bear to look at it; and they walked away. (105)

The stick is the literal embodiment of a 'germ' that has 'blossomed to maturity', displacing the brothers' 'forward visions' with a reminder of the past they have tried so strenuously to delete. Exactly the same imagery is deployed in the story written early in 1891, 'For Conscience' Sake', where the protagonist, Mr Millbourne (the withholding of the first name is appropriate for a character who proves ill-equipped for personal relations) attempts late in life to make up for lost time by offering to marry the woman he had abandoned to single motherhood twenty years earlier. This motivation, which attempts to redeem early mistakes, is common among the late stories, which explore the various ways in which such projects are always based on self-deception. Millbourne's projected marriage goes ahead, but produces disenchantment on both sides, and even threatens the projected marriage of his newly legitimised daughter. The only reparation he can make is disappearance: not only from the lives of his wife and daughter, but also from his own life, since his departure involves a change of name, a change of abode, and even a change of country. This self-deletion is presented as a *fait accompli* in the farewell letter addressed to his wife:

> I have learnt that there are some derelictions of duty which cannot be blotted out by tardy accomplishment. Our evil actions do not remain isolated in the past, waiting only to be reversed: like locomotive plants they spread and reroot, till to destroy the original stem has no material effect in killing them. (73–4)

This resumption of the imagery of furtive growth suggests the impossibility of detecting and acknowledging the constant transformations of memory and desire that undermine any attempt to understand and come to terms with either the self or others.

One of the most revealing aspects of the 1891 stories is this anxiety about partial knowledge. Despite the superficially unifying tendency of late nineteenth-century culture; despite the efficiency of rail networks, postal deliveries and increasingly centralised distribution systems for all kinds of produce, Britain remained fundamentally disconnected in various, sometimes quite profound, ways. The opening of 'The Son's Veto' (December, 1891) is set in a London park on the occasion of a concert organised by a local association for the benefit of an unnamed charity. These circumstances offer a pretext for the narrator to observe that the metropolitan environment is in fact divided into a series of mutually exclusive areas: 'There are worlds within worlds in the great city, and [. . .] nobody outside the immediate district had ever heard of the charity, or the band, or the garden' (35). In social and psychological terms, this makes the London suburb as isolated as Gaymead, the Wessex village that Sophy, the female protagonist, has grown up in. Gaymead is first mentioned as being 'remote', though only forty miles from London. In terms of the distribution of knowledge, both rural Wessex and suburban London are characterised in terms of uncertainty and inaccessibility. The alienating effect of these disconnections is profound enough to be felt even in the imagining of death and resurrection:

> Mr Twycott had never rallied, and now lay in a well-packed cemetery to the south of the great city, where, if all the dead it contained had stood erect and alive, not one would have known him or recognised his name. (42)

Sophy's isolation is deepened by widowhood, which reduces the scope of her involvement in suburban life to that of lonely onlooker: 'bending forward over the window-sill on the first floor, stretching her eyes far up and down the vista of sooty trees, hazy air, and drab house-facades' (42).

Most of the first two pages of the story are concerned with the problems of obtaining and interpreting visual evidence. Sophy is introduced in the very first sentence as a figure seen from behind as she sits in the audience for the concert: 'To the eyes of a man viewing it from behind the nut-brown hair was a wonder and a mystery' (35). This point of view is maintained for long enough to establish the unreliability of deduction based on incomplete, or obstructed, visual data. The curiosity of the onlookers is aroused without being satisfied, and even verbal enquiry produces only vague and inconclusive results: 'She was generally believed to be a woman with a story – an innocent one, but a story of some sort or other' (37).

The story that the emphasis on visual appearance has already connected Sophy with is that of the *Odyssey*, and specifically that of the hapless Penelope, trapped for a period of years in the solitary weaving and unweaving of a tapestry that is worked on during the day and unravelled at night, precisely in order to defer the moment when she must accept one or other of the suitors for her hand in marriage. Unusual emphasis is placed at the beginning of 'The Son's Veto' on the care with which Sophy 'braided', 'twisted', 'coiled' and 'composed' her hair, only to 'demolish' it again 'regularly at bedtime' (35). The irony implicit in this allusion is that while Penelope was anxious to prolong the process, Sophy's story turns around her desire to terminate it. The figure of Sam combines the roles of both suitor and long-lost companion; he is both usurper and the one who keeps faith. The main difference in Sophy's story is the degree of power accorded to the Telemachus figure, the son, who establishes a permanent veto on remarriage. This veto is the measure of his inability to accept a part of his inheritance, the part that troubles his sense of class identity. The narrator's antipathy towards his resistance is suggested by disapproval of the symbolic deferment:

> One could understand such weavings and coilings being wrought to last for a year, or even a calendar month; but that they should be all demolished regularly at bedtime, after a single day of permanence, seemed a reckless waste of fabrication. (35)

By prolonging the process of deferment, the son hopes to fabricate an identity for his mother that will disguise both her class origins and his affiliation to them.

Despite fiction's chronic reliance on the examination of appearances, and despite the intensity of Hardy's emphasis on the operation of the gaze in the first two pages of the story, the possibilities for misinterpretation are insisted on in the hesitant and open-ended way in which interpretation is introduced: 'She fell into reverie, of a somewhat sad kind to all appearance. It might have been assumed that she was wondering . . .' (37). If the deceptive nature of visual evidence means that appearance is no guarantee of identity, the class identity of Sophy is betrayed as soon as she opens her mouth: her first utterance in the story is a grammatical error, which her well-educated son reacts to 'with an impatient fastidiousness that was almost harsh' (37). It is language that reveals her origins, despite the best efforts of husband and son to eradicate the signs of her rustic character; even after fourteen years of training, 'she still held confused ideas on the use of 'was' and 'were'' (41). The dissimulations of husband and son are not restricted to their project of educating the class interloper, they are equally guarded about their own behaviour. The son is actually performing a covert action when he remonstrates with his mother about her speech:

His mother hastily adopted the correction, and did not resent his making it, or retaliate, as she might well have done, by bidding him to wipe that crumby mouth of his, whose condition had been caused by surreptitious attempts to eat a piece of cake without taking it out of the pocket wherein it lay concealed. (37)

The father is much less guileful than the son, but his natural inclination is to shield himself from the possibility of misconstruction through 'withdrawal from outward observation' (39). In this world of mutual aversions, Sophy spends the first two years after the death of her husband ostensibly surveying her suburban neighbourhood, while in fact revisiting in her mind's eye the Gaymead of her childhood: 'still she looked on that suburban road, thinking of the village in which she had been born, and whither she would have gone back – O how gladly! – even to work in the fields' (43). Given the intensity of her yearning, it is unsurprising that the vividness of her imagination should displace her perceptions of her immediate surroundings, a process that is augmented with the fading of daylight. It is precisely under the cover of darkness that the produce of the fields Sophy would now like to work in makes its way past her very house. Because of the desire she now feels for the humblest of objects and occupations, even simple vegetables are surrounded with an aura of the exotic: there are 'bastions' of cabbages, 'walls' of beans and peas, 'pyramids' of turnips, and 'howdahs' of mixed produce' (44).

The extraordinary paradox in Sophy's situation is that her growing ambition to return to the village of her birth throws into reverse the usual relationship between country and city in the inexorable pull towards the urban centres throughout most of the nineteenth century. It was usually the city that held the promise of glamour, wider experience and of a magical change of fortune; but unlike Jude Fawley, Sophy turns back to the country as a potential source of enchantment: 'they had an interest, almost a charm, for Sophy, these semi-rural people and vehicles moving in an urban atmosphere' (44). Nonetheless the material component of her ambition as a country girl to acquire a comfortable position in life has induced in her habits of thought that her son will be able to exploit in preventing her marriage to Sam Hobson. The psychological contradictions that allow for the endless stalemate of the rest of her life are in place in her first conversation with Sam after recognising him in the road outside her London house. She refers to this dwelling place as 'home', but then uses the same word to refer to Gaymead:

'This is my home – for life. The house belongs to me. But I understand – ' She let it out then. 'Yes, Sam. I long for home – *our* home! I *should* like to be there, and never leave it, and die there.' (46)

In the first usage, 'home' means no more than property, possession, asset; but in the second it evokes a sense of belonging that is at its sharpest perhaps in those who have been exiled from their original homes: natives who wish to return. The tension between these two very different constructions on the same word is felt widely in the nineteenth century, but nowhere more keenly than in the West Country (especially Dorset) where especially low incomes and bad housing were responsible for continued migration out of the rural areas.[1]

Sophy's first journey into Covent Garden, seated on the cabbages in the back of Sam's vehicle, is a time of enchantment, with talk of the old days mingling with the illusion of a country drive: 'the air was as fresh as country air at this hour' (47). The experience brings her back to life both physically and emotionally: 'The air and Sam's presence had revived her: her cheeks were quite pink – almost beautiful' (47). This pacific invasion of the city by the country, which romanticises the economic necessity for all the night-time traffic, recalls the interdependence of rural and urban communities in *The Mayor of Casterbridge*. But the mutual responsiveness of farming and trading communities in that novel is shadowed by the antagonisms of a three-tiered social structure that is clearly mapped onto different areas of the town. At the bottom of the social scale are those who inhabit the suburb of Durnover, a literally benighted place, in that all the important business – the illegal activity that enables survival – is conducted at night. In 'The Son's Veto', Hardy simplifies the classification of different social groups, but preserves the temporal and geographical distinctions between the activities of a leisured middle class and the labours of those who provide for them. There is a direct contrast between the nightly cargoes of vegetables and the holiday carriages of the well-to-do enjoying their picnics in a 'lurid July sun' (38):

> Sophy saw the large proportion of boys like her own, in their broad white collars and dwarf hats, and all around the rows of great coaches under which was jumbled the *debris* of luxurious luncheons: bones, pie-crusts, champagne-bottles, glasses, plates, napkins, and the family silver; while on the coaches sat the proud fathers and mothers; but never a poor mother like her. (49)

The cornucopia of vegetables on their way to market suggest productivity and industry, while the piles of leftovers discarded by the picnickers imply waste and excess. It is in the context of such conspicuous consumption, during a public school cricket match at Lord's, that Sophy fails crucially to broach to her son the subject of her intended marriage to Sam. It is the first, critical misgiving on her part that sets the pattern for her chronic failure of nerve. But the decisive factor is the spectacle of glamour by which she is overawed: 'the contrast between her story and the display of fashion' (50).

If this is the first inhibiting factor, a dramatic emphasis on the visual evidence for prosperity, the second is her inability to master the language of privilege: 'Sophy fetched up the sentence that had been already shaped; but she could not get it out' (49–50). Even with education, even with careful preparation, Sophy is unable to give voice to the language that would obliterate the marks of 'home', in the sense that she now holds dear. The word 'obliterate' is actually part of the son's vocabulary; it refers to his intention of keeping his distance from a mother who can only prove a social embarrassment to him: 'Better obliterate her as much as possible' (51). The Latin origin of the word secures the link between the idea of erasure and the expunging of written letters, a link on which Hardy builds powerfully with the circumstance of the mother's illiteracy. Perhaps the most poignant sentence in the entire story is Sophy's final utterance of longing for Sam, couched ineradicably in a grammatical error: ' "Why mayn't I say to Sam that I'll marry him? Why mayn't I?" she would murmur plaintively to herself when nobody was near' (52).

Illiteracy is also at the centre of Hardy's most virtuosic story of 1891, 'On the Western Circuit'. Here the rural character's inability to read and write is paralleled by the sophisticated Londoner's inability to detect the fictional status of the letters written on her behalf. The author of the letters, Edith Harnham, is gradually drawn into an infatuation with Charles Raye by the persuasiveness of her own fiction; such is the power of writing to embody sexual and social desire that she ends up deceiving herself as effectively as she deceives the man in the case. Both are mesmerised by the power of the text more than by physical proximity. For Edith, the seemingly oxymoronic condition of 'vicarious intimacy' (128) is not simply the *impasse* into which her involvement with Raye is going to lead, it is also the starting point for her interest in him. She first observes the flirtation between Raye and Anna from a literal *impasse*, a 'screened nook' (117). It is precisely the predisposition to voyeurism that stimulates her curiosity about Raye and that ensures her continued fascination with him. The patient attentiveness with which the movements of Raye and Anna are described make it clear that she is engrossed in keeping them under close surveillance: 'When they drew near the door of the wine-merchant's house, a comparatively deserted spot by this time, they stood invisible for a little while in the shadow of a wall, where they separated' (117). Vicariousness is not so much the unfortunate barrier to Edith's eventual happiness as a reflex of her overriding psychological compulsion.

Hardy's frequent use of free indirect style in this story provides a short cut to the three characters' habitual modes of thought; but in the case of Edith, this involves the obtrusive use of a vocabulary that seems to have detachment and distance built into it:

> From the first he had attracted her by his looks and voice; by his tender touch; and, with these as *generators*, the writing of letter after letter and the reading of their soft answers had insensibly developed on her side an emotion which fanned his; till there had resulted a *magnetic reciprocity* between the correspondents, notwithstanding that one of them wrote in a character not her own. That he had been able to seduce another woman in two days was his crowning though unrecognized fascination for her as the *she-animal*. (125, emphasis added)

The oddity and awkwardness of this vocabulary suggests an analytical and even a scientific attitude on the part of Edith towards the relationship she is becoming a part of. Curiously enough, there is a complementary inclination in Anna, who is presented initially as a purely physical specimen, really a she-animal, focused almost entirely on sensory appearance: 'the riders were quite fascinated by these equine undulations in this most delightful holiday-game' (111); 'the sighs of the riders were audible' (112); 'she was absolutely unconscious of everything save the act of riding: her features were rapt in an ecstatic dreaminess' (111). What Anna and Edith share is a capacity for obliviousness: Anna's absorption in physical pleasure leads her to ignore her social circumstances, while Edith's absorption in the pleasures of the imagination leads to a parallel neglect of all the ramifications of her situation, as the narrator goes to some pains to make clear:

> Thus it befell that Edith Harnham found herself in the strange position of having to correspond, under no supervision by the real woman, with a man not her husband, in terms which were virtually those of a wife, concerning a corporeal condition that was not Edith's at all. (128)

It is corporeality that removes Anna from an awareness of her surroundings, while it is precisely an absence of the corporeal that places Edith at several removes from the strange 'intimacy' she contrives. None of the main characters – male and female – is able to grasp the reality of other people. This imperceptiveness is perhaps especially marked in the case of Raye. Anna's childishness is made crystal clear to the reader of the story, nowhere more so than in the passage of indirect free style that renders the subject matter of her first conversation with Raye:

> Mrs Harnham was the only friend she had in the world, and being without children had wished to have her near her in preference to anybody else, though she had only lately come; allowed to do almost as she liked, and to have a holiday whenever she asked for it. The husband of this kind young

lady was a rich wine-merchant of the town, but Mrs Harnham did not care much about him. In the daytime you could see the house from where they were talking. She, the speaker, liked Melchester better than the lonely country, and she was going to have a new hat for next Sunday that was to cost fifteen and nine-pence. (113)

The information that Edith is treating Anna as a substitute child is rapidly made congruent with Anna's almost infantile boastfulness and eagerness for self-congratulation. Her naïve excitement at the prospect of a new hat shows her to be completely unsophisticated, while the immature tactlessness of her contempt for Edith's husband is in very sharp contrast with Raye's ultimate expectation of 'tact' in the decisive scene when he discovers her to be capable of nothing more than 'the characters and spelling of a child of eight' (134). If her speech is so ingenuous, the other aspects of her behaviour are if anything even more immature: 'Anna jumped for joy like a little child' (129). She is also clearly obtuse about the realities of desire. When Edith decides she wants to discontinue her writing of the letters, because of its deepening effect on her, Anna's incredulous response is devastatingly naïve: ' "Because of its effect on me." "But it *can't* have any." "Why, child?" "Because you are married already!" said Anna with lucid simplicity' (131). Despite all the evidence for her artlessness, Raye sustains the illusion that Anna is judicious, circumspect and possessed of unusual insight into human nature. This is only possible because of the specific limitations of his own outlook and understanding. It is his occupation as lawyer that has brought him to Melchester, one of the county towns on the 'western circuit' of assize courts. But legal habits of thought and legal language are not confined to his professional activities, they also colour his attitude towards his involvement with Anna, which he reflects on in legal terms and legal phrasing: 'Thoughts of *unpremeditated conduct* [. . .] threw him into a mood of dissatisfied depression' (119; my italics); 'the pseudonym, or rather partial name, that he had given her as his before knowing how far the acquaintance was going to carry him, had been spoken on the spur of the moment, without any *ulterior intention* whatever' (120; my italics). The suspicious use of a pseudonym suggests that Raye might have an instinct for concealment and insincerity. At the very least, it suggests amorality, and is perhaps the acquired behaviour of one expected to plead the case of clients and to attempt to prove their innocence irrespective of their moral liability. The potential for duplicity is evident in Raye's rumination to the effect that 'he could only hope that she might not live to suffer on his account' (119): the contortedness of the construction has the effect of playing down his responsibility for his own actions by attenuating his agency in Anna's story.

The legal mentality operates as a kind of anaesthetic in the early stages of Raye's pursuit of Anna. Edith is similarly inoculated against the moral failures of her own position through a use of cliché: 'what was done could not be undone, and it behoved her now, as Anna's only protector, to help her as much as she could' (124). The proverbial formula followed by the scriptural word ('behoved') is a combination that gives an aura of moral legitimacy to what is the continued practice of deceit. Both Raye and Edith are prevented by their resort to prefabricated language from making sense of Anna as an individual in her own right. They project onto her their expectations of stereotyped behaviour in a mechanical application of habitual phrases. To Raye, Anna is 'pretty rural maiden Anna' (119) and 'his fascinating child of nature' (120), while to Edith, she is a 'poor little creature' (124). Even when Raye is forced to rethink his understanding of Anna after the receipt of the first letter, he achieves nothing more than the adjustment from one stereotype to another, rephrasing his language only to exchange one form of condescension for another: 'It was the most charming little missive he had ever received from woman' (121).

Not only do Raye and Edith tend to regard Anna in stereotypical terms, they also conform to type themselves. Edith, in reflecting on her attraction to Raye, deploys a vocabulary of theatrical role-playing: 'the man being one for whom, mainly through the sympathies involved in playing this part, she cherished a predilection' (128). And Raye uses the same register during his bout of daydreaming in court: 'he would do these things to no purpose, and think how greatly the characters in such scenes contrasted with the pink and breezy Anna' (121). Raye in particular is the subject of extensive taxonomic commentary on the part of the narrator; he is first introduced as 'a gentlemanly young fellow, one of the species found in large towns only' (110). Identification through species suggests an extreme likelihood of behaviour conforming to pattern, as does the categorical scope of the following sentence: 'Indeed, *some would have called him a man not altogether typical* of the middle-class male of a century wherein sordid ambition is the master-passion that seems to be taking the time-honoured place of love' (111, emphasis added). The awkward circumspection of the qualifying phrase does not put up much of a defence against the charge that actually he is fairly typical, and the subsequent phrase referring to Raye as 'the end-of-the-age young man' (118) is quite straightforwardly generic.

The most important thematic emphasis of the story is on the extent to which stereotypes of language and role vitiate the relationships of the main characters. It is not only insincerity in the social uses of language but also the inaccuracies inherent in certain forms of language that limit their perceptions of one another. Paradoxically, it is the ingenuous Anna who provides the most convincing illustration of the fundamental untrustworthiness of language:

> 'All I want is that *niceness* you can so well put into your letters, my dear, dear mistress, and that I can't for the life o' me make up out of my own head, though I mean the same thing and feel it exactly when you've written it down!' (127)

'On the Western Circuit' is a story about the untrustworthiness of language, and yet its own status as written text renders it liable to the same charge of unreliability as the letters that undermine the lives of its three main characters. The reader is bound to wonder whether she or he can trust the language of the narrator of the story. Not only does Hardy fail to allay the reader's mistrust, he accentuates it by providing a volatile, unpredictable, chameleon-like narrator. The narrator's shiftiness seems to be motivated in large part by a corresponding lack of confidence in the abilities of the reader. In its very first sentence, the story introduces a narrator who appears to regard the interpretive abilities of the reader as inadequate: 'The man who played the disturbing part in the two quiet feminine lives hereunder depicted – no great man, in any sense, by the way – first had knowledge of them on an October evening, in the city of Melchester' (109). The parenthetical remark is overemphatic, excess to requirements; it labours to make a point, as if the reader cannot be trusted to draw the right conclusions from the information given. This narratorial obtrusiveness becomes a regular feature of the writing.

The description of Anna as she starts her first conversation with Raye is especially ponderous: 'Unreserved – too unreserved – by nature, she was not experienced enough to be reserved by art' (112). This time the parenthesis does not guide the reader's response, it dictates it. It has to be said that the characteristics of the narrator at this late stage of Hardy's career in prose fiction are disturbingly provocative, challenging, even aggressive. Perhaps the most remarkable narratorial intervention of all comes near the end of the first section of the story, anticipating the sequel to the meeting of Raye and Anna in terms so pessimistic, they appear to dismiss out of hand the necessity for the reader to proceed any further:

> Each time that she approached the half of her orbit that lay nearest him they gazed at each other with smiles, and with that unmistakable expression which means so little at the moment, yet so often leads up to passion, heartache, union, disunion, devotion, overpopulation, drudgery, content, resignation, despair. (113–14)

The progressively generalising sweep of this aside to the reader is fuelled by a ready supply of disillusionment, and even of cynicism. The writing buckles time and time again, even if only momentarily, to the pressure of the narrator's exasperation. There is an unmistakeable world-weariness behind the dogmatic expatiations on typical forms of behaviour, as in the reflection on Anna's being able to speak correct English, even if she cannot write it: 'in which accomplishment Anna showed considerable readiness, *as is not unusual with the illiterate*' (123, emphasis added). If this seems condescending towards the character, and pompous in its buttonholing of the reader, its didacticism is matched by the estimate of Edith's response to Anna's pregnancy: 'Edith Harnham was generous enough to be very far from inclined to cast Anna adrift at this conjuncture. *No true woman ever is so inclined from her own personal point of view*' (126, emphasis added). If the narrator here seems inclined to be generous, like Edith herself, he is also simultaneously throwing down a challenge to all women readers to live up to their 'true' potential. In contrast to these examples of overt opinionation – sometimes even of prejudice – there are other occasions on which the narrator seems vague, uncertain, and even indifferent: 'whether an inkling of Anna's circumstances [her pregnancy] reached the knowledge of Mrs Harnham's husband or not *cannot be said*' (128, emphasis added).

In sum, the narrator of 'On the Western Circuit' is, by turns, domineering, obtrusive, cynical, condescending, prejudiced, opinionated, evasive, negligent, and just downright puzzling. The implied attitude to the reader is on occasion hostile, often resentful, nearly always distrustful. It is almost as if Hardy is taking for granted that his story will be misunderstood. Perhaps this is inevitable given that all of the short stories in *Life's Little Ironies* were written while Hardy was either writing, publishing or dealing with publishers' rejections of, or the critics' responses to, the successive versions of the text that became *Tess of the d'Urbervilles*.

In 1891, the final version was published, but only after the earlier drafts had been rejected, sparking various expressions of frustration and resentment on Hardy's part. In 1890, he had published the essay, 'Candour in English Fiction', a grimly impassioned protest against 'Grundyism' and the role of magazines and circulating libraries in restricting the scope of English fiction to a degree that prevented it from addressing the realities of experience.[2] The essay insists on the necessity for modern fiction to emulate Greek and Shakespearean tragedy in being 'sincere', 'true', 'conscientious', 'accurate', 'honest', 'uncompromising', 'unvarnished', while the existing state of affairs is such as to promote 'falsity', 'censoriousness', 'charlatanry'. Editorial interference produces insincerity in English fiction, which is much narrower in scope than its French counterpart; any attempt to resist the falsifying of the writer's original conception is undermined by public taste: 'To this expansion English society opposes a well-nigh insuperable bar.'³

The pernicious influence of the magazines and lending libraries – orientated towards a family audience – produces a reading public unable to cope with certain kinds of subject matter, untrained in certain methods of reading. Even during the writing of *Tess*, and shortly after the publication of *Wessex Tales*, Hardy had written anxiously about the limitations of the reader catered for by the English book-selling and book-lending industries. In 'The Profitable Reading of Fiction', with its ironic title, he concludes a series of guidances to the would-be reader of contemporary fiction with a crotchety dismissal of those who misread the author's intentions:

> It is unfortunately quite possible to read the most elevating works of imagination in our own or any language, and, by fixing the regard on the wrong sides of the subject, to gather not a grain of wisdom from them, nay, sometimes positive harm. What author has not had his experience of such readers? – the mentally and morally warped ones of both sexes, who will, where practicable, so twist plain and obvious meanings as to see in an honest picture of human nature an attack on religion, morals, or institutions. Truly has it been observed that 'the eye sees that which it brings with it the means of seeing'.⁴

This is a strikingly vehement ending to an essay that is otherwise carefully measured in its calculation of the risks that authors take with their readers. Its sourness can be matched by authorial outbursts at various stages of Hardy's career. One of the most revealing examples of his chronic indignation in this respect is the remarkable authorial note added to the 1912 edition of *The Return of the Native*, which shows Hardy bearing a grudge against readerly incompetence for over thirty years:

> The writer may state here that the original conception of the story did not design a marriage between Thomasin and Venn [. . .]. But certain circumstances of serial publication led to a change of intent.
>
> Readers can therefore choose between the endings, and those with an austere artistic code can assume the more consistent conclusion to be the true one.⁵

The identification of authorial design with truth, and of the conventions of reading promoted by magazines with falsity, is identical to the emphasis placed in both essays published during the writing of *Tess* and its troubled reception by publishers. Hardy agreed to publish drastically bowdlerised versions of *Tess* in the magazines *Graphic* and *Harper's Bazaar*, but was determined keep to his original design for publication in book form.⁶ In order to achieve this, he returned an advance to

Tillotson rather than make the cuts requested; the work was then offered to *Murray's Magazine* and to Macmillan, both of whom rejected it, much to Hardy's fury.[7] When finally published by Osgood, McIlvaine in November 1891, the novel was met with both hostile and ecstatic reviews. Hardy's last-minute decision to add the subtitle 'A Pure Woman', has been seen as a deliberate challenge to the sanctimonious, and it is clearly an act of defiance that shows his willingness to be confrontational with his readers.[8]

It was during the protracted composition and publication of *Tess*, a process that involved the most complex series of revisions and excisions that he had ever undertaken, that Hardy wrote the bulk of the stories that were to appear in *Life's Little Ironies*. The constant readjustment of his sense of the audience he was writing for, a chameleon-like adaptability to different sets of expectations and criteria of acceptability, have left their mark on the narratorial caginess of the stories, which quite frequently betray the impatience that Hardy managed to keep in check while drafting his novels.

Before writing the final two stories, 'The Fiddler of the Reels' (May 1893) and 'An Imaginative Woman' (September 1893), Hardy found time to prepare the first version of his penultimate novel, *The Pursuit of the Well-Beloved*, a text whose preoccupations announce a change of direction in Hardy's understanding of the scope of English fiction. The protagonist, Jocelyn Pierston, becomes obsessed with a woman who is supposed to be embodied and re-embodied in three successive generations of the same family. The three versions of the same woman, Avice I, Avice II and Avice III, advertise a major shift in Hardy's conception of character; he has changed his focus from character as individual to character as type, as example of a class, or of a race, and even of a species. Human longevity is no longer the dominant scale of significance in the novel, as it is for the *Bildungsroman* and related forms of fiction.

The narrative is not concerned to trace the development of character, through a series of different experiences, but is drawn towards the repetition of actions and the duplication of identities. It reflects that aspect of *Tess of the d'Urbervilles* concerned with the extent to which Tess can be thought of as 'acting the part of someone just like her', because in some degree her career is determined by genetics, by her membership of a family that has produced similar types among Tess's ancestors and will produce similar types again among future generations. The emphasis upon inheritance, reaching back to the past, and projecting forward into the future, is an important element in the composition of Hardy's two stories of 1893. If 'A Tragedy of Two Ambitions', the earliest story in *Life's Little Ironies*, is haunted by the idea of the burden of the past, both 'The Fiddler of the Reels' and 'An Imaginative Woman' are troubled by the question of responsibility towards the future, particularly in respect of the treatment of children by their parents.

'The Fiddler of the Reels' begins with a reference to parentage, but not to the parenting of the main characters, Car'line Aspent and Wat Ollamoor, who fail in the offices of fatherhood and motherhood, nor to the parenting of Ned Hipcroft who is robbed of the step-daughter he loves so keenly; in a story that returns constantly to the question of parental responsibilities, it is remarkable that the first use of the word 'parent' does not refer to a person or a duty, but to an event: the Great Exhibition of 1851, which is characterised as the 'parent of them all', the first and most definitive in the series of exhibitions and world's fairs that have followed in its wake ever since.

The Great Exhibition figures in the introductory section of the story as the progenitor of modernity: it announces a cataclysmic change, a seismic shift, in awareness of the culture of modernity which, above all, operates on an international scale and in an immanent fashion. The all-pervasiveness of new styles of thought is expressed through the invasion of the English language by the adjective 'exhibition': 'It was "exhibition" hat, "exhibition" razor-strop, "exhibition" watch; nay, even "exhibition" weather, "exhibition" spirits, sweethearts, babies, wives – for the time' (165). Hardy's catalogue of objects transmutes rapidly into the annexing of general conditions and even of human relations; if British culture is suddenly unified by the enthusiasm for the exhibition, this is because everything is commodified by its influence, even children. The abruptness with which Victorian society is catapulted into the culture of modernity – nowhere more abruptly than in South Wessex, apparently – is characterised by a use of metaphors drawn from one of Hardy's most favoured discursive fields, that of geology:

> For South Wessex, the year formed in many ways an extraordinary chronological frontier of transit-line, at which there occurred what one might call a precipice in Time. As in a geological 'fault', we had presented to us a sudden bringing of ancient and modern into absolute contact, such as probably in no other single year since the Conquest was ever witnessed in this part of the country. (165)

Despite the sudden and irreversible spreading of a homogeneous culture of modernity throughout the entire country, the forcing of connections is successful in geographical terms, but disorientating in historical terms: the juxtaposing of ancient and modern is experienced as a kind of rupture, a break in continuity, rather than the secure transmission of a legacy from one generation to the next. Among the three main characters, the 'respectable mechanic', Ned Hipcroft, is not only drawn into the advent of the modern, but contributes to its making, through his direct involvement in the construction of the Crystal Palace, while his rival for Car'line's affections, the amoral Wat Ollamoor, is closely associated with an archaic past, with the residual memory of a folk culture embodied in 'country jigs, reels, and "Favourite Quick Steps" of the last century' (167).

However, Ollamoor's relationship with tradition is skewed, opportunistic, productive of distortion. While the 'peculiar and personal quality' of his fiddling is compared to the style of a 'moving preacher', the effects of his playing are opposite to those of a religious discourse, aimed as they are at seduction rather than moral instruction. It is stressed that he has 'never bowed a note of church-music from his birth' (167), and is thus set apart from the principal milieu for music-making in Hardy's fiction as a whole, the church gallery in which local musicians contribute to one of the most important communal activities of the rural scene. Far from promoting a sense of harmony and teamwork, Ollamoor's playing induces a sense of disharmony, of contradictory impulses and of disorientation in the listener: 'Presently the aching of the heart seized her simultaneously with a wild desire to glide airily in the mazes of an infinite dance' (168). Whereas the music of groups such as that which plays in Mellstock church in *Under the Greenwood Tree* helps one to keep one's place, in both space and time, the effect of Ollamoor's playing is to make one lose one's place and one's self-control, to be left in a maze.

From the start, it is made clear that the appeal of Wat's music is chiefly seen in its effect on children, and this seems to be preparing the way for an association between his character and the figure of the Pied Piper: 'He could make any child in the parish, who was at all sensitive to music, burst into tears in a few minutes' (167). This form of seduction is left unexamined, as if its folkloric origins alone give it enough force to be convincing, whereas the less frequent and correspondingly more spectacular influence exerted over 'the souls of grown-up persons' (168) apparently requires systematic explanation, even though this is difficult to manage: 'it would require a neurologist to fully explain' (169). The narrator deploys a language of scientific exactitude in describing Car'line's reactions to the power of Wat's fiddling: 'she would start from her seat in the chimney-corner as if she had received a galvanic shock, and spring convulsively towards the ceiling' (169). This attempt to bring the phenomenon within the scope of modern, rational terms of analysis, regarding Car'line almost as the subject of a practical experiment, remains on the outside of her experience. The failure of scientific language reflects the failure of the 'respectable mechanic' Ned, builder of the modern world, to make any headway against the primeval compulsions bound up in Wat's music:

> Though her father supported him and her sister supported him, he could not play the fiddle so as to draw your soul out of your body like a spider's thread, as Mop did, till you felt as limp as withywind and yearned for something to cling to. (170)

This remarkable sentence begins by identifying with Ned's position, but in the sudden switch to the second person changes to a vivid rendering of Car'line's experience. The evocation of a close familiarity with local flora and fauna, and the use of dialect, strengthen the sense of opposition between the traditional and the new-fangled, between forms of experience that are deeply rooted on the one hand and superficially acquired on the other. The disorientating rapidity with which traditional modes of thought and feeling are overtaken by modernity is illustrated by a dramatic reorganisation in the relations of time and space.

The events of the story take place over a period of four or five years; at the beginning of this period, the railway from South Wessex to London has not yet been built, so that Ned's journey to the capital takes him no less than six days on foot; four years later, when the railway has been completed, he is joined by Car'line and her child in a matter of hours. The extension of the rail network coincides with the construction of the Crystal Palace, with the result that the story juxtaposes a rural setting in which the distance between the villages of Mellstock and Stickleford is significant, and the international setting of the Great Exhibition to which 'people were flocking ... from all parts of the globe' (172). In the letter Car'line sends to Ned before rejoining him, she promises to 'make up for lost time', and there is an important sense in which the story as a whole is primarily concerned with this possibility, that in the chronological 'precipice' referred to in the second paragraph there is a general loss of certain ways of experiencing time. If Ned had remained in Wessex, he would have passed the time with Car'line in a way and according to a tempo different from that of his life in London; but by the end of the story, Wessex is already beginning to catch up.

At this point, the most important loss of all occurs, the loss of the child, Carry, and what this means is the loss of anticipated time, time to be spent together by mother, child and step-father; it is one version of the future that does not happen. Hardy is imagining, across the 'fault-line' of history, alternative lives, alternative stories for the child: a prospect of life with her biological father, atavistic, backward-looking, a future that seems like a mirror of the past; or a life with her adoptive father that is in tune with the nineteenth-century ideology of progress. The second version of the story is forfeited, while the first version is simply not given, which means that both versions are effectively suspended. Whatever regrets Hardy may have for the 'lost time' of Wessex, these are put into conflict with his evident distrust of the 'rogue' Ollamoor, while his apprehensiveness with regard to the rushing onset of modernity is qualified by his evident approval of the moral character of Hipcroft.

The structural ambiguity of these arrangements, which pivot around Hardy's sense of the contradictory movement of history – daunting expectation with the fear of loss, and tantalising memory with dreams of the path not taken – seems to be encapsulated in the strange episode in which Car'line glimpses the image of Wat in a mirror at the Great Exhibition. It is far from certain that Wat is there, or that Car'line is not imagining his appearance, but the insertion of this archaic figure within the epitome of the modern is emblematic of the story's narrative and conceptual dilemma, which makes it so unwilling to take responsibility for its own projected future.

The second story from 1893, 'An Imaginative Woman', concerns a similar irresponsibility towards both cultural and familial legacies. The title's reference to imaginativeness is paradoxical, perhaps even sarcastic, since the story examines different types of imaginativeness, ranging from excessive fantasising to a capacity for empathy, while making it clear that the eponymous heroine, Ella Marchmill, represents only a narrow band of meanings within this spectrum.

What gives the subject matter particular resonance is its implication for Hardy's attitude towards his own story-telling craft and its reception. Nowhere in the story is there any suggestion of excessive imaginativeness on Ella's part before her marriage to William Marchmill. Yet after it, she depends on the resources of her imagination so completely that she seems incapable of performing even the most straightforward of tasks, such as walking, without the comfort of escaping into a book, and into the 'reverie' that reading induces in her. The huge gulf that has developed between husband and wife does not derive from spectacular differences of temperament or outlook but from seemingly unobtrusive beginnings in divergences of 'taste' and 'fancy', which the narrator refers to oxymoronically as 'those smallest, greatest particulars' (4).

Marchmill himself is more companionable and sensitive than Ella gives him credit for. He enjoys the trust, and earns the affection and admiration, of newspaper editors and landscape painters, suggesting that his openness to social contacts has more than a merely economic character, and that he has genuine curiosity about other walks of life and other ways of seeing the world; unlike Ella, whose inability to take account of others' points of view leads her into the oxymoronic belief that Trewe is her 'beloved though as yet unseen one' (22). Marchmill's unexpected return on the night set aside for her enjoyment of Trewe's photograph is attributed to an empathetic tenderness: 'he stooped and kissed her. "I wanted to be with you tonight" ' (18).

The repeated emphasis on his commercial success, chiefly in the use of the epithet 'thriving', might seem to invite a recoil on the part of the fastidious reader, given the nature of his business, which is armaments manufacturing. However, the narrator does not concede the high ground to Ella's very different sense of priorities; her poetic activities are described as 'browbeaten efforts' in a 'pathetic trade', which locates her cultural aspirations within the same sphere as her husband's more pragmatic ambitions. It is true that there is a readiness on the part of the narrator to deploy sarcasm in implying the husband's moral condition; his 'soul' is said to be constantly in his gunmaking business.

But there is an equal ironicalness in the way that Ella's deliberate obtuseness with regard to the nature of this business, and her refusal to acquire a 'detailed knowledge' of what it involves, is attributed to her humaneness, rather than to egoism or amorality. Her aversion to knowing more becomes the pretext for an ironic reversal when Robert Trewe, the object of her subsequent obsession, chooses a revolver as the instrument of his suicide. The depth of Ella's egoism is suggested vividly by the extent to which her behaviour differs from that of the rest of her family after they move into their new lodgings. Husband and children depart promptly for pier and beach, while Ella remains behind to admire herself in a mirror: 'testing the reflecting powers of the mirror in the wardrobe door' (6). The vocabulary here shows the narrator amusing himself with the absurd notion that Ella is conducting a scientific experiment rather than indulging her vanity, and makes clear her facility for self-deception.

The change of lodgings is said to involve the Marchmill family 'taking possession' of Coburg House. The concept of appropriation is at the centre of the story's concerns. There is an especially persistent use of a vocabulary of property ownership in reference to married relationships. This is uncertain in provenance; it could reflect the narrator's cynicism, but equally it could be traced to Ella's own cast of mind, or 'cast of soul', as the phrasing has it (5). The translation of 'getting married' into 'getting life-leased' and of her 'husband' into 'her proprietor' probably strikes the reader as typical of Hardy's own disenchantment with the institution of marriage; however, it is at least technically possible that Ella herself thinks in these terms, which would make any married relationship the pretext for off-setting fantasies.

It is particularly revealing that the fantasy at the centre of 'An Imaginative Woman' has its basis in Ella's adoption of a building, and most particularly of a room, of which neither she nor Robert Trewe are proprietors, but which they both imprint with their own meanings. Trewe actually scribbles ideas for his poems directly on the walls, while Ella weaves a fiction of possession that is totally one-sided. The building itself is first referred to as visually ambivalent, as a construction whose pretensions can be seen through:

> The spot was bright and lively now; but in winter it became necessary to place sandbags against the door, and to stuff up the keyhole against the wind and rain, which had worn the paint so thin that the priming and knotting showed through. (5)

Trewe's preference for wintry weather is proportional to its effectiveness in reducing the possibilities of human contact: 'he cares more to be here when the south-westerly gales are beating against the door, and the sea washes over the Parade, and there's not a soul in the place, than he does now in the season' (6). The desire to be rid of others qualifies Trewe's superficially romantic interest in the turbulent sea, conventionally symbolic of a passionate nature. And, of course, his relationship with tempestuous conditions is one of contemplation only; he remains inside in the company of his books, a collection of specifically 'correct' editions.

The same imagery applies to Ella's yearning for a greater emotional fluidity: for a 'congenial channel in which to let flow her painfully embayed emotions, whose former limpidity and sparkle seemed departing in the stagnation caused by the routine of a practical household' (7). The irony here is that Ella's daydreams begin to flow in the very middle-class context of a seaside resort, precisely the kind of place where the sea is conveniently 'embayed'.

Both Ella and Trewe are in fact inhibited less by external conventions than by the *embourgeoisement* of their own imaginations. As poets they are both dependent on second-hand experiences and emotions; tragedy, for example, is not an element they see the potential for in their own lives, but something they read about in the newspapers: 'Both of them had, in fact, been struck by a tragic incident reported in the daily papers, and had used it simultaneously as an inspiration' (7–8). The resulting poems are published in the same magazine, and actually on the same page, the one in large, the other in 'smallish' print, indicating different levels of status and accomplishment.

But even if Ella's efforts are inferior to Trewe's (we have no means of checking) they are deliberate imitations, precisely modelled on the male poet's example, and reflect certain aspects of his work with disconcerting accuracy. Ella's chosen pseudonym, 'John Ivy', expresses the parasitical nature of her relationship with Trewe's work. Imitation concentrates on what is most imitable, reproducible, and hence what is most reductive and commonplace in the prior text; in some sense, it concentrates on what is most commodifiable, most conducive to magazine publication, an aspect of writing that is underlined in the reference to both poets as 'fellow-tradesmen' (9).

The lack of dignity in Ella's attempts to cancel out the differences between her own work and Trewe's is captured in the moment of farce that arises from her trying on his mackintosh and cap, the decidedly unromantic garments that she equates, absurdly, with the 'mantle of Elijah' (12). But even this pantomime does not satisfy her urge for identification, which reaches its furthest point in her re-staging of Trewe's physical posture while writing on the wall: 'He must have put up his hand so – with the pencil in it. Yes, the writing was sideways, as it would be if executed by one who extended his arm thus' (17). The deictics, 'thus' and 'so', and the exploratory movement of the syntax inject the moment with a dramatic immediacy which only underscores the inadequacy of Ella's imaginative projection, which does not respond creatively to Trewe's example but seeks merely to replicate it.

Trewe's work is characterised by the narrator as excessive ('luxuriant rather than finished') and unconsidered ('little attracted by excellences of form and rhythm apart from content'), suggesting that Ella's will be even more self-indulgent. It would seem that her writing verses produces nothing of value in and for itself but serves mainly as a form of therapy, a possibility echoed in the way her husband places literature and medical treatment in the same category: 'Her husband had paid the publisher's bill with the doctor's' (9). The extent to which Ella and Trewe are confined by their own perceptions of the world is nothing short of pathological. Neither possesses that genuine imaginativeness that allows them to achieve insight into the experience of others. Trewe is so unprepared for alternative ways of seeing his own work, that the adverse criticism of one reviewer is enough to drive him to suicide, a reaction that is so pathological, one cannot help reflecting on the authorial attitude towards a character who caves in after exposure to only a tiny proportion of the opposition that Hardy had to contend with himself.

But the story is at its most severe in offering a critique of egoism and emotional atrophy, not in respect of Ella's failure to achieve romantic attachment, but in her chilling detachment from the claims of her own children. While Trewe's legacy is a set of poems written to an 'imaginary woman' (25), Ella's is the diversion of her love away from living, breathing children towards an entirely 'imaginary man'. The paradox inherent in the title of the story is that neither Trewe nor Ella is truly 'imaginative'. Until the very end, the children are barely noticed; they are never individualised, but are referred to sweepingly in formulations expressive of Ella's boredom at the prospect of motherhood, which to her is one of the root causes of her emotional stagnation, 'stagnation caused by the routine of a practical household and the gloom of bearing children to a commonplace father' (7). It is not clear whether it is the narrator's sourness or Ella's own repugnance that motivates the characterisation of motherhood as a condition in which she is a 'mere multiplier of her kind' (9). The lack of emotional warmth towards the children is correlative with her absorption by 'an inner flame which left her hardly conscious of what was proceeding around her' (11); this is the fantasy that she is twice said to be 'possessed by', even though its subject is 'a man she had never seen' (11).

Indifference to the children modulates gradually into culpable negligence; when they rush in from the beach with wet stockings, she takes the measure of her growing disaffection: 'she could not feel that she cared about them half as much as usual' (14). At this point, the narrator mixes condescension with derision in accounting for Ella's distraction: 'so aching was her erratic little heart' (14), and is at his most robustly sarcastic in mocking her double standards:

> She knew [Trewe's] thoughts and feelings as well as she knew her own; they were, in fact, the self-same thoughts and feelings as hers, which her husband distinctly lacked; perhaps luckily for himself, considering that he had to provide the family expenses. (16)

The closest that Ella gets to a physical reality in her relationship with Trewe is in tracing the outlines of his writing on the wall above her bed; and yet this writing is itself characterised as immaterial in outlook, conjuring up an attitude to the physical world that is as dismissive as that of the poet described in Shelley's *Prometheus Unbound*. Hardy quotes the lines that celebrate the poet's ability to create 'Forms more real than living man, Nurslings of immortality' (17). Even in Shelley, the use of the word 'nurslings' invites criticism of the artist who would turn his back on real children in order to nurture the progeny of his imagination, but in 'An Imaginative Woman', with its constant registration of parental neglect, the word has special weight.

The other conspicuous literary allusion in the story takes the form of a quotation from Rossetti's sonnet 'Stillborn Love': 'The hour which might have been yet might not be, / Which man's and woman's heart conceived and bore / Yet whereof life was barren' (26). The whole burden of

Rossetti's poem is the symbolic equation between frustrated love and the casting out of a child, the 'Bondchild of all consummate joys set free'. In 'An Imaginative Woman' this equation is literalised as a set of stark alternatives, with the story culminating in the brutal rejection of Ella's fourth child. Even though Marchmill's detection of a family resemblance between the suicide Trewe and this unfortunate child is posited on the basis of a mere superstition, the psychological power motivating the superstition, and the moral culpability it appears to embody, is prepared for in Ella's anticipation of meeting, finally, with the object of her desires as the arrival of a 'pregnant day and hour' (22).

Marchmill's chilling rejection of the boy who has already lost one parent, shows that although he has coped better than his wife with the reality of other people, his respect for the views of others is in the end motivated by the fear of being rejected himself, rather than by any ethical regard. This is not to forget that Ella is equally unreliable as a parent, having turned away from emotional commitment to the children on several occasions: 'she had a sudden sense of disgust at being reminded how plain-looking they were, like their father' (24). The occasion referred to here is when she draws back from 'unnecessarily kissing' them, in marked contrast to her obsessive kissing of the lock of hair from the head of the dead poet, and her exclamation that she 'would have suffered shame and scorn, would have lived and died, for him!' (26).

When she lies dying in the aftermath of giving birth to her fourth child, it is unclear whether the ascription of 'unnecessary life' to the infant is a mark of her own resentfulness or of the narrator's disillusionment. Either way, the dismissal of children themselves, and of the attention paid to them, as 'unnecessary' mounts a direct challenge to the reader's ethical judgement. It is remarkable that, in both stories from 1893 included in *Life's Little Ironies*, there should be such a pronounced emphasis on the issues of parental responsibility and on the betrayal of art, whose products are conceived of as the children of the imagination.

Notes

1. K.D.M. Snell, *Annals of the Labouring Poor: Social Change and Agrarian England, 1660–1900* (Cambridge: Cambridge University Press, 1985), Chapter 8 *passim*.
2. 'Candour in English Fiction', *New Review* (January 1890), pp. 15–21.
3. 'Candour in English Fiction', collected in *Thomas Hardy's Personal Writings*, ed. Harold Orel (London: Macmillan, 1967), p. 128.
4. 'The Profitable Reading of Fiction', ibid., p. 125.

5. Thomas Hardy, *The Return of the Native* (London: Macmillan, 1949), p. 473.
6. Claire Tomalin, *Thomas Hardy: The Time-Torn Man* (London: Viking, 2006), p. 228.
7. Ralph Pite, *Thomas Hardy: The Guarded Life* (London: Picador, 2006), p. 306.
8. Michael Millgate, *Thomas Hardy: A Biography* (Oxford: Oxford University Press, 1985), pp. 318–19.

Chapter 4

A Changed Man

Hardy's final volume of short stories, *A Changed Man*, brings together work written at various points during a period of almost twenty years, between 1881 and 1900, and this helps to give it a more miscellaneous character than the other three books discussed in this study. That said, it is also the case that six of the stories represent Hardy's final attempts at literary fiction, being written between 1893 and 1900, and this chronological proximity is clearly a factor in their related choices of subject and setting.

This chapter will focus on the group of late stories, with occasional reference back to the earlier work, beginning with the 1885 text, 'A Tryst at an Ancient Earthwork', since this provides a convenient stepping-stone to discussion of the themes of historical retrieval and the ethos of keeping faith with the past. The story is unusual in Hardy's output in its sustained use of the present tense, which is paradoxical given its imaginative fascination with events up to 2,000 years old. The 'tryst' referred to in the title is a meeting between the narrator and an antiquarian who proposes to excavate a part of the Iron Age hill-fort where the action is set.

The meeting has to take place at night, since the digging is actually illegal and can only be carried out under cover of darkness. The illegality is compounded by the removal from the site of a Roman statuette, thus provoking questions about the value of historical enquiry, whether carried out by archaeologists or by writers; whether the recovery of historical evidence is carried out with respect and integrity, or whether it becomes the merest pretext for selfish appropriation.[1] The ambivalence of such forays into the past is underlined by the fact that, even when the majority of the finds are re-interred, this is sometimes too late to prevent their crumbling to dust. Whenever the past is revisited, its character is altered forever afterwards. This practical lesson for the archaeologist has unforeseeable moral complications for the protagonists of the late stories, in their attempts to revise the history of their personal relations.

At the same time, the history of the Iron-age fort in its treatment by the local community over the intervening period of 2,000 years has been one of continuous depredation:

> It is a long-violated retreat; all its corner-stones, plinths, and architraves were carried away to build neighbouring villages even before mediaeval or modern history began. Many a block which once may have helped to form a bastion here rests now in broken and diminished shape as part of the chimney-corner of some shepherd's cottage within the distant horizon, and the corner-stones of this heathen altar may form the base-course of some adjoining village church. (177)

This tradition of interference, borrowing and incorporation places the original character of the historical object at a greater remove, but also gives it a new lease of life in a different form, by bringing it literally closer to home. The opening descriptions of the story are sharply reminiscent of the panoramic survey of Egdon Heath at the start of *The Return of the Native*, published only five years earlier in 1878. Both landscapes are defined by archaeological characteristics, in the case of Egdon Heath by the frequent presence of round barrows, excavated amateurishly and raided to provide household ornaments in the shape of Bronze Age funerary urns. In the novel, Hardy seems mesmerised by these acts of simultaneous piety and impiety, by the installation of totems that superstition gives pride of place to, while also travestying their original purpose. Both the novel and the short story seem to accept the compromise of history implicit in the afterlives of objects, remaining sceptical about the ability of the professional to detach the original object from the accretions of subsequent usage.

The narrator of 'A Tryst at an Ancient Earthwork' uses the present tense to make especially vivid his account of the difficulties of scaling the ramparts, in a way that clearly evokes the imagined experience of the Roman invaders. The use of the present tense dramatises the effect of eliding the whole of time between that of the Romans and the present day, while the narrator speculates on the impossibility of ever bridging this gap except in fiction, in the opportunities of storytelling that he simultaneously performs and cancels out:

> Who was the man that said, 'Let it be built here!' – not on that hill yonder, or on that ridge behind, but on this best spot of all? Whether he were some great one of the Belgae, or of the Durotriges, or the travelling engineer of Britain's united tribes, must for ever remain time's secret; his form cannot be realized, nor his countenance, nor the tongue that he spoke, when he set down his foot with a thud and said, 'Let it be here!' (178)

This narrative wager, which professes ignorance while also indulging in a fantasy of what might have been, is essentially what haunts the narrators of the late stories, once it has been transposed into a different key. At its simplest, it takes the form of narrating a secret or hidden history that is either submerged or contradicted by the official account. This is the case in the 1893 story, 'Master John Horseleigh, Knight', which is designed to reveal the truth about the marital status of the eponymous knight, whose name has been recorded in the Havenpool marriage register as that of the husband of one Edith Stocker, despite the universal belief that he was married to a woman by the name of Phelipson, who bore him three children. Horseleigh's public reputation links him in marriage to a gentlewoman who has no legal right to be called his wife, while his authentic marriage to the tradesman's daughter, Edith, is kept secret. Hardy is less interested in the legality of these relationships than in the extent to which either of them is based on 'loving-kindness', a concept and a phrase that preoccupies him in this period of increasing antipathy towards marriage as an institution. It is, of course, the socially inadmissible relationship that is the locus both for 'loving-kindness' and for the inevitably tragic outcome.

The story is given the character of an oral supplement to the official written account of the marriage register, and is supposedly relayed by a character identified only in parenthesis as 'the thin-faced gentleman', implying a frame narrative that is not in fact provided. This failure to specify either the teller of the tale or the situation in which it is told suggests that the sole purpose behind the delegation of narrative responsibility is to emphasise its orality. There is a similar friction between different registers in the description of Sir John's country estate of Clyfton Horseleigh, with the lengthy excerpt from the sixteenth-century document reflecting an evident admiration on the writer's part for the scale and variety of Sir John's possessions, while the concomitant response on the reader's part is likely to align them with the rising indignation of Edith's brother, Roger, who sees in all this prosperity the likelihood that his sister is being deceived and his family dishonoured.

The narrative provides an historical perspective on this powerful sense of social inequality by emphasising how radically patterns of trade and occupation and the distribution of wealth have changed since the sixteenth century, and in particular how the Clyfton Horseleigh estate has all but vanished: 'Of this fine manorial residence hardly a trace now remains' (237). Horseleigh's descendants have all died out, while the story of Edith Stocker continues to be told. The opposition between written and oral, official and unofficial, and between authority and resistance to that authority is subject to delicate negotiation between the individual narrator and the material supplied by communal tradition, in a process of what the story in its closing phase refers to as 'corroboration'.

The majority of stories in *A Changed Man* begin by advertising their dependence on this process. 'A Committee-Man of "The Terror"' (1895), written two years after 'Master John Horseleigh, Knight' is particularly elaborate in its specification of the complexities of reading and writing, telling and listening involved in the recording and transmission of stories:

> The writer, quite a youth, was present merely as a listener. The conversation proceeded from general subjects to particular, until old Mrs. H——, whose memory was as perfect at eighty as it had ever been in her life, interested us all by the obvious fidelity with which she repeated a story many times related to her by her mother when our aged friend was a girl [. . .].
>
> 'I wrote it down in the shape of a story some years ago, just after my mother's death,' said Mrs. H——. 'It is locked up in my desk there now.'
>
> 'Read it!' said we.
>
> 'No,' said she; 'the light is bad, and I can remember it well enough, word for word, flourishes and all.' (213)

Although the present version of the story has been written down, it is based on the narrator's memory of listening in his youth to the oral rendering of a written account that had been committed to memory, and the version then performed had itself been committed to paper several years after the last possible occasion on which it had been transmitted orally from another source. Even before the main events of the story begin to be unfolded, the scope for misinterpretation, for accretion and omission, is made to seem dizzying, in a text which focuses on the capacity of individual memory to evolve in conformity with a changing ratio of desires and inhibitions. The main characters, the 'Committee-Man' of the title and a certain 'Mademoiselle V——', both exiles from Bonapartist France, represent total opposites on the political spectrum. While he had been a willing instrument of the revolutionary government, she had been a member of one of the aristocratic families that fell victim to its purges. Despite the enormous gulf between them – political, religious, emotional – and despite the determined resistance of the female protagonist, they end up being powerfully attracted to one another, almost as if the magnetic bearings of their natures are suddenly reversed. They even make preparations for marriage before both, opposing principle to emotion, decide independently to rescind their promises to each other. The story reaches a climax with the remarkable scene in which both attempt to leave the 'old-fashioned watering-place' in which the action is set, by boarding what turns out to be exactly the same carriage bound for London, a circumstance that is recognised only subliminally by the heroine when her resolve fails half-way through the journey:

> Abandoning her place in the coach with the precipitancy that had characterized her taking it, she waited till the vehicle had driven off, something in the departing shapes of the outside passengers against the starlit sky giving her a start, as she afterwards remembered. (226)

But although she succumbs to emotion, he holds to principle, departing from her life, from the story and from the compass of the narrator's knowledge. The story ends with a curious folding-back upon the conditions in which it began, almost as if to parenthesise itself:

> Recovering from her stupor, Mademoiselle V— bethought herself again of her employer, Mrs. Newbold, whom recent events had estranged. To that lady she went with a full heart, and explained everything. Mrs. Newbold kept to herself her opinion of the episode, and reinstalled the deserted bride in her old position as governess to the family. (228)

In the terms whose implications are explored by Hardy throughout the 1880s and 1890s, the extraordinary events of the story are seen retrospectively as a 'mere interlude' in the ordinary course of the protagonists' lives, despite the fact that they involve a far greater revolution in the realm of feeling than they do in the world of political events. At the most intense phase of their connection, neither of the two lovers keeps faith with the past, in the sense that both override the internalised moral codes of their respective backgrounds, in the attempt to come together without prejudice. In the conception of the Committee-Man, this requires an effective deletion of the self: 'Why not, as he had suggested, bury memories, and inaugurate a new era by this union?' (226). Obliterating the past and starting history again from scratch, as if from the year zero, is precisely what the revolutionary government had tried to accomplish. But for Hardy it is precisely the burying and un-burying of memories, the sedimentation of experience and the excavation of earlier strata that make 'interludes' a psychological impossibility.[2] Despite the strict chronological succession of events, and the containment of this unlikely *rapprochement* in a brief episode, it is the subsequent tension between alternative lives that persists in the memory:

> As her hair grew white, and her features pinched, Mademoiselle V- would wonder what nook of the world contained her lover, if he lived, and if by any chance she might see him again. But when, some time in the 'twenties, death came to her, at no great age, that outline against the stars of the morning remained as the last glimpse she ever obtained of her family's foe and her once affianced husband. (228)

It is the dual possibility of commitment to friend and enemy, of the coexistence in a single relationship of both love and hate, that motivates the constant imagining of divergent and convergent destinies in the late short stories, and that finds its most intense expression in respect of the most binding commitment of all, that of marriage.

At the same time, Hardy is also fascinated by those junction-points in historical time that divide families and nations interchangeably into groups of friends and enemies and that cast shadows over recorded history with the shapes of what might have been, or what might still be. In 'A Committee-Man of "The Terror" ', the cultural parenthesis within which two French people are drawn towards one another against the relatively hostile background of an English coastal town is accentuated by the royal visit calling for increased security measures:

> The King's awkward preference for a part of the coast in such dangerous proximity to France made it necessary that a strict military vigilance should be exercised to guard the royal residents. Half-a-dozen frigates were every night posted in a line across the bay, and two lines of sentinels, one at the water's edge and another behind the Esplanade, occupied the whole sea-front after every night. (222–3)

A considerable number of the short stories are set early in the nineteenth century at a time when invasion was a constant threat and the possibility of altering the direction of history was a pressure not just on individual psychology but on collective awareness.

In the following year, 1896, Hardy composed 'The Duke's Reappearance'. This ghost story accepted for publication in the *Saturday Review* both revisits an historical moment when successful invasion might have altered the subsequent development of English culture, and imagines the possibility that the Duke of Monmouth might not have died when commonly supposed, but survived to leave open the possibility of a parallel history, a different interpretation of the same events. The story recounts how the yeoman, Christopher Swetman, unwittingly gives shelter to the Duke of Monmouth in the aftermath of the latter's defeat. Swetman is represented as being friendly to the Duke's cause, 'in his secret heart' (249) although he has abstained from any direct involvement in the conflict: 'Christopher Swetman had weighed both sides of the question, and had remained at home' (248). It is this 'weighing both sides' which proves impossible to sustain, not only at moments of national crisis, but in the regulation of his own household and its 'unbroken traditions' (247).

The Duke's claim to the throne rests on his status as illegitimate son of Charles II, a condition that does not present an obstruction to Swetman's loyalty, although bastardy would present insuperable difficulties to inheritance in the traditions of his own bourgeois family, as his fierce protection of his daughter's honour makes clear. It is because Monmouth tries to seduce her that Swetman insists on ejecting him from the family home, and this expulsion leads to the Duke's capture and reported execution. It is only after this denouement that Swetman identifies Monmouth as the stranger who had sought his protection, and the discovery leads him to revise his attitude towards his daughter and the value of her modesty: 'On the girls coming up to him he said, "Get away with ye, wenches: I fear you have been the ruin of an unfortunate man!"' (254). What is judged acceptable in the context of affairs of state is unacceptable to the morality of family life; in the best traditions of Greek tragedy, loyalty towards one is rendered incompatible with loyalty towards the other. It is for this reason that Swetman needs so desperately to believe that Monmouth does not lose his life as a result of forfeiting his protection, but survives against all the odds: 'His belief in the rumour that Monmouth lived, like that of thousands of others, continued to the end of his days' (255–6).

In the night after Monmouth's execution, an apparition closely resembling the Duke visits Swetman's bedchamber in order to take away the belongings Monmouth had left there, including the sword that seems to authenticate his paternity. While the conventions of sensational magazine fiction predispose the reader to identify this apparition as Monmouth's ghost, Swetman's conviction that his nocturnal visitor must have been the Duke in person is in itself a measure of the psychological strain under which he has been placed. The supernatural in Hardy is often correlative with insupportable tension between desire and inhibition, and while the story supports equally the inference of ghost, physical intruder and delusion, both supernatural and naturalistic interpretations relate less systematically to the story's development than the intelligibility derived from a psychological reading.

The conflict between a sense of piety towards the time and place of origins and the awareness of wider contexts for experience and judgement is deeply rooted in Hardy's fiction, which often explores its effects through scenarios of exile and return. But the alienation of the returning native, living mentally within more than one geographical reality and aware of different ways of measuring duration, becomes routinised in the late stories, which show a fascination with the most commonplace basis for negotiating the difficulties of separation and reunion in the figure of the soldier home on leave. John Peck has argued how the novels *Far from the Madding Crowd* (1874) and *The Trumpet Major* (1880) reflect

> a deep division within the national character between aggressive, military impulses and peaceful, domestic impulses. It is a tension that Hardy [. . .] is perhaps the first to detect and explore. The problem in essence, is how does the country reconcile its new-found enthusiasm for militarism with its, by now well-established, liberal tradition? How can the inward-looking insularity of the latter be combined with the outward-looking aggression of the former?[3]

The stories in *A Changed Man* do not match this emphasis on the alternatives of aggression and pacification, despite their frequent references to invasion, but if anything they amplify the distinction between inward-looking and outward-looking priorities and values. The three stories, 'The Grave by the Handpost' (1897), 'Enter a Dragoon' (1899) and 'A Changed Man' (1900), all concern the demobilisation of soldiers and the contrast between domestic virtues and the glamorous risks of travel.

'The Grave by the Handpost' touches on the military careers of two separate generations of soldiers in the relationship between father and son, Sergeant Holway and Luke Holway. Their experience of the army is radically different, the father serving during peacetime and encouraging his son, to the point of forcing him, to join the army despite – and even because of – the outbreak of war with France:

> 'Trade is coming to nothing in these days,' he said. 'And if the war with the French lasts, as it will, trade will be still worse. The army, Luke – that's the thing for 'ee. 'Twas the making of me, and 'twill be the making of you. I hadn't half such a chance as you'll have in these splendid hotter times.' (132)

But this prediction, while accurate in some respects, does not allow for the misery and squalor of active service at a time of hostilities, and Luke's military experience induces both depression and violent resentment of his father's interference in his choice of a career. When he is at his lowest ebb, he sends a letter of recrimination that devastates the old man. The letter is soon regretted, but too late to prevent the retired soldier from committing suicide. Luke's eventual return to his Wessex home is timed to coincide with his father's burial, at a crossroads high on a ridge dividing two villages, in the 'grave by the handpost'. The ignominious circumstances of this interment outside of hallowed ground distress the son almost as much as his role in precipitating the tragedy, and the rest of the story is concerned with his efforts to have the body exhumed and removed to a final resting-place in one of the local churchyards.

The story begins with a paragraph in which the narrator muses on the wisdom of disinterment – not, this time, of a body, but of 'memories of village history' (129). The reasons for this caution over the unearthing of buried memories is not immediately apparent, but as the opening scene unfolds vividly with an account of the Chalk-Newton choristers venturing out into the winter night to sing carols, the narration is punctuated with a few self-reflexive queries about the plausibility of the story, noting that certain details have been derived from the 'testimony of William Dewy' (129), while others survive, 'according to the assertions of several' (130). When the choristers catch sight of the gravediggers' lantern – without knowing yet what they are looking at – they begin to draw conclusions based on 'the probability of the light having origin in an event of which rumours had reached them' (131). The piecing together of evidence from different sources, which may or may not be reliable, affects every stage of the construction placed on events.

Storytelling at this phase of Hardy's activity as a writer of fiction is an inherently second-hand activity, always posthumous to an imagined point of origin. A first-hand account would have a greater claim to authenticity and more substance than the mere 'whispers of that spot' (129) that the narrator argues have a 'claim to be preserved' (129). The status of the written and published version of these 'whispers', which suggest a living, breathing connection, however attenuated, with the events they refer to, is hedged about with questions of answerability, in view of the significance of documentation in a story in which tragedy arises precisely from the reading of a written text. The letter is predicated on absence, which means that it is read in circumstances that preclude enquiries about meaning and intention; the reader has no means of eliciting reassurance or qualification. Luke purposes to redeem in some measure the catastrophe of his first written text by composing another, the inscription that is to be carved on his father's gravestone:

HERE LYETH THE BODY OF SAMUEL HOLWAY, LATE SERGEANT IN HIS MAJESTY'S – D REGIMENT OF FOOT, WHO DEPARTED THIS LIFE DECEMBER THE 20TH, 180-. ERECTED BY L. H.
'I AM NOT WORTHY TO BE CALLED THY SON.' (138)

But this text is also destined to fend for itself in his absence. He is called abroad to the war in Spain, leaving instructions for the exhumation and reburial, and paying in advance both for this and for the gravestone. The response to his decisiveness and resolution is failure on the part of his 'friends', the members of the Chalk-Newton choir, to realise his wishes. The remainder of the story is a chronicle of negligence and inaction, with the rector and sexton finding insuperable difficulties in the alarming possibility that the corpse has had a stake driven through it during the first burial. The headstone is deposited first in the sexton's outhouse, then among the bushes at the bottom of his garden, where it is broken up by a falling tree and finally buried under leaves and mould. The entire shameful episode is the result of connivance. Blame cannot be laid at the door of specific individuals but is the outcome of collective inertia. Just as the story itself is not the responsibility of any single narrator but is a composite of various 'whispers', so the abandonment of Luke Holway's narrative of his relationship with his father involves the corroboration of all those who have been charged with upholding it, in what is a virtual conspiracy of silence. The story gravitates towards the representing of dereliction in every sense.

When Holway returns for the second time, he is of course unable to find anywhere in the churchyard 'the memorial bearing the inscription: "I AM NOT WORTHY TO BE CALLED THY SON"' (140). By this time, his military achievements at Waterloo and other campaigns have made him literally unrecognisable to the residents of Chalk-Newton and Sidlinch. The outward change is an index of the extent to which he has rendered himself worthy of his father's name, while it is his 'friends' who have rendered themselves unworthy in his absence. When he goes out of his way to avoid the painful reminder of the roadside grave, the vocabulary of the description draws attention to the moral evasiveness of those who have left it untouched: 'he got over the hedge and wandered deviously through the ploughed fields to avoid the scene' (140). While Luke has been devious only in the technical sense of making a deviation, it is precisely the way in which the choir's wandering progress at the start of the story has become the prelude to their straying morally by the end, that confirms the need for caution in the narrator's disinterment of the 'memories of village history'. The mutual corroboration of different accounts can mask a complicity of misrepresentation, as the story's shocking denouement throws into relief. It is partly the dereliction of his textual intentions that leads the younger Holway to commit suicide also: 'Sergeant-Major Holway had been found shot through the head by his own hand at the cross-roads in Long Ash Lane where his father lay buried' (141). And there is surely an embittered authorial inflection in the stark account of tragic irony that rounds off this confabulation of whispers:

> On the table in the cottage he had left a piece of paper, on which he had written his wish that he might be buried at the Cross beside his father. But the paper was accidentally swept to the floor, and overlooked till after his funeral, which took place in the ordinary way in the churchyard. (141)

Luke composes no fewer than three texts whose reception histories are likely to inhibit authorial ambitions. It is initially the outward-looking experience of the soldier that leads him to miscalculate the effect that his words will have at home, while the choral nature of village opinion – represented by the musicians of the church choir who also function consensually like the chorus in a Greek tragedy – appears to give the inward-looking experience of the stay-at-homes a certain value by reason of custom and communality. By the end of the story, however, the sympathetic bias has been altered to reflect the evolution of Luke's character in an ever wider scope of interactions, while the narrow focus of Chalk-Newton life has become associated with impasse and moral decay.

With 'Enter a Dragoon' (1899), this dynamic is almost reversed. The story introduces the idea of dereliction, or dilapidation, in the very first paragraph, with its description of the demolition of a house 'with whose outside aspect' the narrator claims he has 'long been familiar' (145). The opportunity of viewing the interior of this condemned structure enables him to project into its settings the details of a number of stories he has become aware of over the years, although he is quite clear about the fact that his knowledge of the house and of the family histories of those who have lived in it is at best patchy, indirect and incomplete; he is able to 'reckon only those which had come to my own knowledge. And no doubt there were many more of which I had never heard' (114). This general disclaimer is in tune with a narrative method based on supposition and opportunistic observation.

The retrospective account that fills out the main body of the story is introduced through another choral focus, in the description of a mixed group of men and women whose words are not addressed directly to the narrator – and through him, to the reader – but overheard and interpreted, with attendant reception issues: 'From their words any casual listener might have gathered information of what had occurred' (146). The neighbours are speculating about the reasons for the 'commotion' that has erupted inside the house; by taking turns, they piece together an account of the romantic history of the daughter of the household, Selina Paddock. Selina is the recipient of another life-changing letter, also from a soldier, who is none other than the former fiancé she had believed killed at the Battle of the Alma two years before. In the intervening period she has become engaged to yet another man, a local miller with the apt name of Bartholomew Miller. The letter has the effect of a disinterment, effectively bringing the dead back to life, presenting Selina with an apparent dilemma which, however, she has little difficulty in resolving. Almost automatically, she reverts to the soldier's prior claim on her affections, partly in order to legitimise her son, Johnny, who has been without a father until now.

Despite the fact that she has agreed to marry the miller in a week's time, all the months and years devoted to building an alternative to her life with Corporal, now Sergeant-Major, Clark, are deleted in an instant, in her eagerness to share the wishful thinking of her first love that 'time shuts up together, and all between then and now seems not to have been!' (157). Hardy's usual apprehensiveness about the ethical dangers of living in terms of interludes comes into play in the graphic reminder of passing time and its transformations supplied by the image of the rotted 'mummy' of a wedding-cake. Clark himself refers to it as a 'withered corpse' (157) and, despite the comparative youth and freshness of Selina, it serves as a reminder of the penalties of trying to turn the clock back no less than Miss Havisham's great bride-cake in Dickens' *Great Expectations*.

Clark's disinterment is brief indeed. On the very evening of his return to Mellstock, he collapses and dies after overstretching himself during a celebratory dance. Selina loses him for a second time, but does not console herself with the substitute miller, choosing instead to adopt the name of Clark and the role of widow, moving to Chalk-Newton and supporting herself through the sale of fruit and vegetables. The miller remains hopeful for a while, but eventually marries a prosperous dairyman's daughter in another part of the county. The closing scene features Selina and her son in the course of one of their regular visits to the graveyard where Clark is buried. The final twist of the plot, reminiscent of 'The Withered Arm' in its combination of *peripeteia* and *anagnorisis*, reveals the existence of another wife, legally married to Clark in the immediate aftermath of his return from the Crimea. Selina finds this woman engaged in another species of disinterment:

> On reaching the churchyard and turning the corner towards the spot as usual, she was surprised to perceive another woman, also apparently a respectable widow, and with a tiny boy by her side, bending over Clark's turf, and spudding up with the point of her umbrella some ivy-roots that Selina had reverently planted there to form an evergreen mantle over the mound. (166)

The ivy symbolises attachment, fidelity, constancy, all translated into forms of self-deception by the disclosure of another narrative in which Clark has played a central part. The setting for this has been in Yorkshire, sufficiently distant from Wessex and foreign enough to the Wessex mentality for even the most familiar significations to be made strange; 'I am sorry I pulled up your ivy-roots', admits the Yorkshire wife, 'but that common sort of ivy is considered a weed in my part of the country' (166).

The negotiation between inward-looking and outward-looking values and traditions is extremely complex, and even confusing, for the reader of 'Enter a Dragoon'. Selina's decision to revert to her original marriage plans, when given the chance, provides some moral restitution and social respectability within the neighbourhood of Mellstock – it promises to defuse the kind of prurience that is hinted at in the gossip overheard at the beginning of the story. But at least a part of Selina's decision is owing to the glamour by association with soldiering that her marriage to Clark will bring, as well as the enlargement of scope that comes with the mobility of a soldier's life, the recognition it implies of a more worldly and sophisticated attitude towards personal relationships than is ever likely in the rural backwaters of Wessex. On the other hand, it is precisely the nomadic basis of military life that permits a character like Clark to propose marriage to different women living in different places, and to abandon not one but both of them when it suits him to do so.

The initial impression of Clark is that he has returned to Mellstock in good faith, that his behaviour is honourable, and that it is Selina who has been comparatively fickle in finding a pretext to transfer her affections to an alternative lover. The list of the dead at the Battle of the Alma specifically included a James Clark rather than a John Clark, but Selina assumes a mistake has been made, despite the common incidence of the surname. But with each successive disclosure of his recent history, the reader's respect for the soldier diminishes in proportion as their compassion for Selina is likely to increase, the more because her loyalty towards his memory becomes increasingly pathetic. By the end of the story, the soldier's dismissal of the insular viewpoint begins to seem little more than an excuse for uncontrolled selfishness. On the other hand, his competitor in love, the prosaic miller, is too disenchantingly pragmatic to capture the moral high ground that insularity seems entitled to. His devotion to Selina has a kind of dogged charm in the early stages of the narration, until it becomes clear that his systematic passivity during the wholesale reorganisation of his life by Clark and Selina has a supine and even ignoble aspect. His ultimatum to Selina after Clark's death does not serve to romanticise his steadfastness, but casts him in the role of creditor demanding a return for his investment; now that Selina has nothing left to bargain with, he does not bother to disguise the fact that his primary objectives in getting married are logistical:

> 'The truth is, that mother is growing old, and I am away from home a good deal, so that it is almost necessary there should be another person in the house with her besides me. That's the practical consideration which forces me to think of taking a wife'. (165)

The reader's orientation towards these alternative contexts for the characters' attitudes and behaviour, balancing the claims of locality against the perception of anomalous activity in the wider world, is made progressively insecure. The introversion of rooted communities is challenged not only by the cosmopolitan outlook of the soldier, and vice versa, but by the unfamiliar traditions of equivalent communities in other parts of Britain, where the same language has a different accent, and where the hierarchies of value have a different ecology. The dialogical potential of this lack of congruency seems capable of almost infinite ramification, in the hesitations and qualifications of authority that accompany narratorial admission of indebtedness to a variety of sources of information, different histories of transmission, a mixed economy of interpretations. Hardy's vision of England in *Life's Little Ironies* and *A Changed Man* is of a culture divided between traditional and modern, local and national, native and foreign conventions of meaning. The profound sense of disconnection between individuals that governs the roughly-splinted character of many of his plots is amplified in the disarticulation of relationships between speaker and listener, writer and reader, storyteller and literary artist.

Nowhere is the janus-faced character of this vision more apparent than in Hardy's only twentieth-century fictional text, which is also, incidentally, one of his finest short stories, 'A Changed Man' (1900). The story is pervaded by images of division and separation. It begins, typically for a Hardy short story, by establishing its own distance from the events that it narrates, attributing its knowledge of them to a source well-placed but ill-fitted to understand the quality of the experience examined. The source is a well-to-do invalid living at the 'top of the town' in Casterbridge; a stranger to romantic attachment himself, he is proportionally inquisitive about its action upon others. This voyeuristic tendency is reinforced by the vantage-point from which he surveys the citizenry of Casterbridge, an 'oriel window on the first floor, whence could be obtained a raking view of the High Street' (3). The source gathers information, therefore, under panoptical conditions, his physical proximity to those he observes being dislocated by his first-floor elevation and by their unconscious availability for inspection. The narration is predicated on a combination of proximity and remoteness, contiguity and separation. Remarkably, the first paragraph expands the vista opened up by this view of Casterbridge, until it reaches as far as London, and a specific venue that makes its extension to the symbolic centre of English culture simultaneously a reminder of its international context:

> Looking eastward down the town from the same favoured gazebo, the long perspective of houses declined and dwindled till they merged in the highway across the moor. The white riband of road disappeared over Grey's Bridge a quarter of a mile off, to plunge into innumerable rustic windings, shy shades, and solitary undulations up hill and down dale for one hundred and twenty miles till it exhibited itself at Hyde Park Corner as a smooth bland surface in touch with a busy and fashionable world. (3)

These two sentences carefully take the measure of the geographical distance between province and metropolis, but they also make an instantaneous link between the oriel and the Crystal Palace in their shared emphasis on exhibition, exposure, transparency. What puts them 'in touch' with one another is their immunity to touch, their refusal of human contact even though this contact has given them their subject matter. Even before the 'actors' in the story have been mentioned, their world is presented as a mixture of connections and disconnections, affecting the relations between local, national and international and the mutual interventions of the traditional and the modern.

The Great Exhibition had been introduced at the beginning of 'The Fiddler of the Reels' as marking both the scale and the suddenness of the transition between traditional and modern, and the nature of its role in drawing together the imaginations of those who were geographically dispersed was conveyed in a geological metaphor, encoding the actions of time in arrangements of space. Similar principles operate in the figuring of change in 'A Changed Man', where the characters are forced to cope with major transitions in their own lives, with comprehensive redefinitions of the basis and scope of their interactions with others. The pivotal change is the conversion of a dashing and extroverted cavalry captain into a dedicated and self-sacrificing curate. The early descriptions of Maumbry suggest a volatile nature, an ambivalence that allows for change but gives no sign of his eventual steadfastness:

> Maumbry showed himself to be a handsome man of twenty-eight or thirty, with an attractive hint of wickedness in his manner that was sure to make him adorable with good young women. The large dark eyes that lit his pale face expressed this wickedness strongly, though such was the adaptability of their rays that one could think they might have expressed sadness or seriousness just as readily, if he had had a mind for such. (4–5)

This perception is biased by the source narrator's own indecisiveness of outlook, by his cultivation of a frame of mind that takes pleasure from the suspension of choice; one of the reasons he attends the wedding of Maumbry and Laura is 'a subconsciousness that, though the couple might be happy in their experiences, there was sufficient possibility of their being otherwise to colour the musings of an onlooker with a pleasing pathos of conjecture' (7–8). The source narrator's chronic passivity militates against his understanding of Maumbry's eventual commitment to wholesale change. The change is not merely from a military to a pacific outlook, but involves a fundamental shift in his attitude towards community and the nature of his obligation towards it. Both professionally, and from habit, the cavalryman looks beyond the concerns of those he lives among, while the clergyman's activities are quite precisely circumscribed by the needs of his parishioners.

The source narrator's position is one of structural neutrality, engaging with neither of these sets of relations. His dilatoriness is epitomised in the inscription of a poem – a rather snide variation on the conventions of the epithalamion – on a blank page of his prayer-book. Besides its passionless insipidity, this poem reveals, in the circularity of its form, an essentially paralysed attitude towards the consequences of choice, the temporal perspective of the *rite de passage*:

> AT A HASTY WEDDING
> (*Triolet*)
> If hours be years the twain are blest,
>   For now they solace swift desire.
>   By lifelong ties that tether zest
> If hours be years. The twain are blest
> Do eastern suns slope never west.
>   Nor pallid ashes follow fire.
> If hours be years the twain are blest
>   For now they solace swift desire. (8)

The slightly absurd knowingness of the poem – its patronising attitude towards the bride and groom, whose staying power gets no credit – is founded on the assumption that humanity is incurably fickle, and that its motives are always mixed; it does not conceive of the possibility of principled change, and of the necessity to confront and live with that kind of change. What is moving about the story of Maumbry and Laura is its recognition of the complexity of marriages that have to accommodate quite profound alterations in the terms of agreement between partners, resulting from what amounts to an effective change of personality. When Maumbry becomes a curate, there is no way back to the glamorous excitements of the army life that Laura entered into with him, but for a while she tries to recover certain aspects of what attracted her to that life, by carrying on an affair with another soldier. Their relationship fails, however, and continues to fail despite the second chance it is given, because of Laura's eventual acceptance of the other elements in her relationship with Maumbry that have nothing to do with his having been a soldier.

The muted ending, muted partly because the source narrator has become bored by the turn of events, may seem to consign Laura rather dismally to the pathos of widowed isolation, but in doing so it also endorses the depth and strength of the bond that still connects her to her husband.[4] Hardy is fascinated by the way in which both the lives of individuals, and the lives of communities, can sometimes rise above the upheavals that mark the transition from one major phase of existence to another, while continuing to find meaning and purpose in the connections that survive, slender though these sometimes are.

The major rupture in the relationship of Maumbry and Laura is a temporal one, splitting the history of their marriage into two very different stages. But the sense of estrangement that this gives rise to is plotted repeatedly in terms of spatial gaps and barriers. When Maumbry becomes a curate, he is assigned to the Durnover quarter of Casterbridge, an area divided by poverty from the rest of the town, with landmarks distinguished by reference to this awareness of social quarantine; the critics of his sermons meet at 'the White Hart – an inn standing at the dividing-line between the poor quarter aforesaid and the fashionable quarter of Maumbry's former triumphs' (14). When an epidemic of cholera breaks out in Casterbridge, Maumbry remains in Durnover, while Laura is evacuated to a village near Budmouth Regis.

It is here that she starts the relationship with Vannicock that threatens to separate her permanently from her husband. Her infrequent meetings with Maumbry take place on the summit of a 'dividing hill' (17), where a convenient wall provides an extra barrier between them (health precautions serving to underline the emotional obstruction). This self-same venue becomes the setting for her final assignation with Vannicock, the point of departure for a new life, at the precise spot 'where the old and new roads diverge' (19). But they do not get very far in their journey before encountering Maumbry near the symbolically-named Standfast Corner, where he is engaged in the exhausting task of boiling the infected linen of those who have contracted the disease. This vividly evoked scene proves a turning-point for Laura, and remains in her memory ever afterwards:

> They followed on, and came up to where a vast copper was set in the open air. Here the linen was boiled and disinfected. By the light of the lanterns Laura discovered that her husband was standing by the copper, and that it was he who unloaded the barrow and immersed its contents. The night was so calm and muggy that the conversation by the copper reached her ears.
> 'Are there many more loads tonight?'
> 'There's the clothes o' they that died this afternoon, sir. But that might bide till tomorrow, for you must be tired out.'
> 'We'll do it at once, for I can't ask anybody else to undertake it. Overturn that load on the grass and fetch the rest.'
> The man did so and went off with the barrow. Maumbry paused for a moment to wipe his face, and resumed his homely drudgery amid this squalid and reeking scene, pressing down and stirring the contents of the copper with what looked like an old rolling-pin. The steam therefrom, laden with death, travelled in a low trail across the meadow. (19–20)

The real power of this scene is that it represents a commitment to human contact, to the importance of connection, at all costs, at the risk even of death. It is the most thorough endorsement of the 'touch' referred to at the beginning of the story in its total absence from the experience of the source narrator, and in the abstract conquering of distance that is one of the defining novelties of modernity. In a matter of a few hours, Laura goes from wanting to put as much distance as possible between herself and her husband to one where her commitment to him is more intense than it ever has been. This is expressed physically not in a romantic way, but through participation in what his life, his changed life, has come to mean, even though this places her in harm's way. In the event, she escapes the disease, while he does not.

Maumbry's death is not part of any moral scheme, or system of rewards and punishments, but a mere fluke, an accident of the environment in which he has placed himself.[5] Despite the shocking brevity of their reunion – 'Two days later he lay in his coffin' (22) – Laura holds onto its meaning, the memory of the time and place of her reconnection with him overriding the physical presence of Vannicock:

> What had come between them? No living person. They had been lovers. There was now no material obstacle whatever to their union. But there was the insistent shadow of that unconscious one; the thin figure of him, moving to and fro in front of the ghastly furnace in the gloom of Durnover Moor. (23)

'A Changed Man' provides a remarkable summation of Hardy's concerns in the short story to explore the crisis of relations between local and general, rural and urban, in the ever-widening impact of industrial modernity. It recognises that the experience of conflicting perceptions and values, some becoming obsolete, some emerging into view, is not only unavoidable, but also structural. Perhaps above all, it engages with the difficulty of interpreting and relaying this complex situation, grasping the fact that with each passing moment, subjective insight into historical change becomes second-hand, surviving only in partial form that needs to be reconfigured for future generations, future readerships. And in this respect, it is precisely the opportunity represented by short fiction, with its roots in the situation of the storyteller, and its trajectory leading to the most concentrated and intricate forms of literary prose, that Hardy resorts to for some of the purest and most heady distillations of his vision.

Notes

1. Julian Moynahan and Kristin Brady prefer to keep the two professions separate: 'The descriptive passages set up, as Julian Moynahan has suggested, an implicit contrast between the narrator and the archaeologist – the one able to unearth the past with his imagination, the other interested in its present form as "portable property" and a proof for his private theory.'

Kristin Brady, *The Short Stories of Thomas Hardy: Tales of Past and Present* (London: Macmillan, 1982), p. 171.
2. It was less than a month after first publication of the story that Hardy made his observation on the stratification of the past in the diary entry for January 1897 already mentioned in Chapter 1 (p. 30).
3. John Peck, *War, the Army and Victorian Literature* (London: Macmillan, 1998), pp. xi–xii.
4. Laura's persistence is all the more impressive given the fact that Hardy's original model for the figure of Maumbry, the Rev. Henry Moule, actually survived his involvement in the cholera epidemic of 1854 in his parish of Fordingbridge. See Martin Ray, *Thomas Hardy: A Textual Study of the Short Stories* (Aldershot: Ashgate, 1997), pp. 267–8.
5. Compare Valerie Shaw's comment: 'Many of Hardy's shorter pieces take the basic ingredients of a romantic love plot and then dispose them in such a way as to undermine conventional views about "right choices" and the equation of "moral" behaviour with happiness'. *The Short Story: A Critical Introduction* (London: Longman, 1983), p. 219.

Select Bibliography

All works of prose fiction by Hardy are from the Macmillan Library Edition unless otherwise stated.

Allen, Grant, 'Aesthetic Evolution in Man', *Mind*, V, No. 20, October 1880, pp. 445–64.
Armstrong, Tim, *Haunted Hardy: Poetry, History, Memory* (Basingstoke: Palgrave, 2000).
Beer, Gillian, *Darwin's Plots: Evolutionary Narrative in Darwin, George Eliot and Nineteenth-Century Fiction* (London: Ark Paperbacks, [1983] 1985).
Benjamin, Walter, *Illuminations*, ed. and intro. Hannah Arendt, trans. H. Zohn (London: Fontana, 1973). This translation originally published in 1968 by Harcourt, Brace and World, New York.
Boumelha, Penny, *Thomas Hardy and Women: Sexual Ideology and Narrative Form* (Brighton, East Sussex: Harvester Press, 1982).
Brady, Kristin, *The Short Stories of Thomas Hardy: Tales of Past and Present* (London: Macmillan, 1982).
Clarke, Graham (ed.), *Thomas Hardy: Critical Assessments*, 4 vols (Mountfield, East Sussex: Helm Information Ltd, 1993).
Cox, R. (ed.), *Thomas Hardy: The Critical Heritage* (London: Routledge and Kegan Paul, 1970).
Darwin, Charles, *The Descent of Man, and Selection in Relation to Sex*, ed. and intro. James Moore and Adrian Desmond (London: Penguin Books, [1871] 2004).
Dunn, Douglas, 'Thomas Hardy's Narrative Art: The Poems and Short Stories', Chapter 9 in *The Achievement of Thomas Hardy*, ed. Phillip Mallett (Basingstoke: Macmillan, 2000), pp. 137–54.
Ebbatson, Roger, ' "The Withered Arm" and History', *Critical Survey* 5:2, 1993, pp. 131–5.
Flower, Newman, *Just As It Happened* (London: Cassell, 1950).
Galton, Francis, *Hereditary Genius: An Inquiry into Its Laws and Consequences* (London: Macmillan, 1869).
Gatrell, Simon, *Hardy the Creator: A Textual Biography* (Oxford: Clarendon Press, 1988).

Gilmartin, Sophie, *Ancestry and Narrative in Nineteenth-century British Literature: Blood Relations from Edgeworth to Hardy* (Cambridge: Cambridge University Press, 1998).
—, 'Geology, Genealogy and Church Restoration in Hardy's Writing', Chapter 2 in *The Achievement of Thomas Hardy*, ed. Phillip Mallett (Basingstoke: Macmillan, 2000), pp. 22–40.
Gittings, Robert, *Young Thomas Hardy* (Harmondsworth: Penguin Books Ltd, [1975] 1986).
—, *Thomas Hardy's Later Years* (Boston: Little, Brown & Company, 1978).
Hardy, Florence Emily, *The Early Life of Thomas Hardy, 1840–1891* (London: Macmillan, 1928).
—, *The Later Years of Thomas Hardy, 1892–1928* (London: Macmillan, 1930).
Hardy, Thomas, 'Candour in English Fiction', *New Review*, January 1890, pp. 15–21. Collected in *Thomas Hardy's Personal Writings*, ed. Harold Orel (London: Macmillan, 1967), pp. 125–33.
—, *A Changed Man and Other Tales* ([1913] 1951).
—, *The Collected Letters of Thomas Hardy*, ed. Richard Little Purdy and Michael Millgate, 7 vols (Oxford: Oxford University Press, 1978–88).
—, *The Complete Poems of Thomas Hardy*, ed. James Gibson, New Wessex edition (London: Macmillan, [1976] 1979).
—, 'The Dorsetshire Labourer', *Longman's Magazine*, July 1883, pp. 252–69. Reprinted in *Thomas Hardy's Personal Writings*, ed. Harold Orel (London: Macmillan, 1967), pp. 168–89.
—, *Far From the Madding Crowd* ([1874] 1949).
—, *A Group of Noble Dames* ([1891] 1952).
—, *An Indiscretion in the Life of an Heiress, and Other Stories*, ed. Pamela Dalziel (Oxford: Oxford University Press, [1994] 1998).
—, *Jude the Obscure* ([1896] 1951).
—, *The Life and Death of the Mayor of Casterbridge: A Story of a Man of Character* ([1886] 1950).
—, *The Life and Work of Thomas Hardy*, ed. Michael Millgate (Basingstoke: Macmillan, [1984] 1989).
—, *Life's Little Ironies*, ed. Alan Manford, intro. Norman Page (Oxford: Oxford University Press, [1894] 1996).
—, *Life's Little Ironies: A Set of Tales with Some Colloquial Sketches Entitled A Few Crusted Characters* ([1894] 1952).
—, *The Literary Notebooks of Thomas Hardy*, ed. Lennart A. Bjork, 2 vols (London: Macmillan, 1985).
—, *A Pair of Blue Eyes* ([1873] 1952).
—, *The Personal Notebooks of Thomas Hardy*, ed. Richard H. Taylor (London: Macmillan, 1979).
—, 'Plots for Five Unpublished Short Stories', *London Magazine* (5:11), 1958. pp. 33–45.
—, 'Preface' to *Far from the Madding Crowd* (1874; Wessex Edition, II, 1912). Collected in *Thomas Hardy's Personal Writings*, ed. Harold Orel (London: Macmillan, 1967), pp. 8–11.
—, 'The Profitable Reading of Fiction', *Forum*, New York, March 1888, pp. 57–70. Collected in *Thomas Hardy's Personal Writings*, ed. Harold Orel (London: Macmillan, 1967), pp. 110–25.

—, *The Return of the Native* ([1878] 1949).
—, *Tess of the d'Urbervilles: A Pure Woman* ([1891] 1949).
Hardy, Thomas, *The Trumpet Major: John Loveday A Soldier in the War with Buonaparte and Robert his Brother First Mate in the Merchant Service, A Tale* ([1880] 1950).
—, *Under the Greenwood Tree or The Mellstock Quire: A Rural Painting of the Dutch School* (London: Macmillan, [1872] 1949).
—, *Two on a Tower* ([1882] 1952).
—, *The Well-Beloved: A Sketch of a Temperament* ([1897] 1952).
—, *Wessex Tales* ([1888] 1952).
—, *Wessex Tales*, ed. with intro. and notes by Kathryn R. King (Oxford: Oxford University Press, [1888] 1991).
—, *The Woodlanders* ([1887] 1949). Hutchins, John, *The History and Antiquities of the County of Dorset*, 4 vols, ed. William Shipp and James Whitworth Hodson; 3rd edn intro. by R. Douch (East Ardsley: Classical County Histories, [1861–70] 1973).
Humphry, Mrs., *Manners for Women* (Exeter: Webb and Bower Ltd., 1979) [Facsimile reprint of: 1st ed. London: J. Bowden, 1897].
Irwin, Michael, *Reading Hardy's Landscapes* (Basingstoke: Macmillan, 2000).
Johnson, Suzanne R., 'Another Historic Channel Crossing: Hardy's "A Tradition of Eighteen Hundred and Four" ', *Thomas Hardy Journal* (11:1), February 1995, pp. 43–50.
King, Kathryn R., 'Hardy's "A Tradition of Eighteen Hundred and Four" and "The Anxiety of Invention" ', *Thomas Hardy Journal* (8:2), May 1992.
Kramer, Dale (ed.), *The Cambridge Companion to Thomas Hardy* (Cambridge: Cambridge University Press, 1999).
Lea, Hermann, *Thomas Hardy through the Camera's Eye*, No. 20 of *Monographs for the Study of the Life, Times and Works of Thomas Hardy*, 72 monographs (St Peter Port, Guernsey: Toucan Press, 1964).
—, *Thomas Hardy's Wessex* (London: Macmillan, 1913).
Lindgren, Charlotte, 'Thomas Hardy: Grim Facts and Local Lore', *The Thomas Hardy Journal* (1:3), October 1985, pp. 18–27.
Mallett, Phillip (ed.), *The Achievement of Thomas Hardy* (Basingstoke: Macmillan, 2000).
—, 'Noticing Things: Hardy and the Nature of Nature', Chapter 10 in *The Achievement of Thomas Hardy*, ed. Phillip Mallett (Basingstoke: Macmillan, 2000), pp. 155–70.
Marroni, Francesco, 'The Negation of Eros in *Barbara of the House of Grebe*', *The Thomas Hardy Journal* (10:1), February 1994, pp. 33–41.
Miller, J. Hillis, *Ariadne's Thread* (New Haven, CT: Yale University Press, 1992).
—, *Thomas Hardy: Distance and Desire* (Cambridge, MA: The Belknap Press of Harvard University Press, 1970).
—, *Fiction and Repetition: Seven English Novels* (Cambridge, MA: Harvard University Press, 1982).
—, *Topographies* (Stanford, CA: Stanford University Press, 1995).
Millgate, Michael, *Thomas Hardy: A Biography* (Oxford: Oxford University Press, [1982] 1985).
Moretti, Franco, *Atlas of the European Novel, 1800–1900* (London: Verso, 1998).

Morgan, Rosemarie, *Women and Sexuality in the Novels of Thomas Hardy* (London: Routledge, 1988).
Morrell, Roy, *Thomas Hardy: The Will and the Way* (Kuala Lumpur: University of Malaya Press, 1965).
Orel, Harold (ed.), *Thomas Hardy's Personal Writings* (London: Macmillan, 1967).
O'Toole, Tess, *Genealogy and Fiction in Hardy: Family Lineage and Narrative Lines* (Basingstoke: Macmillan, 1997).
Page, Norman, 'Hardy's Short Stories: A Reconsideration', *Studies in Short Fiction*, Newberry, SC, 11, 1974, pp. 75–84.
—, *Thomas Hardy: The Complete Stories* (London: Dent, 1996).
—, *Thomas Hardy: The Writer and his Background* (London: Bell and Hyman, 1980).
Peck, John, *War, the Army and Victorian Literature* (Basingstoke: Macmillan, 1998).
Pite, Ralph, *Hardy's Geography: Wessex and the Regional Novel* (Basingstoke: Palgrave, 2002).
—, *Thomas Hardy: The Guarded Life* (London: Picador, 2006).
Prentiss, Norman D., 'The Poetics of Interruption in Hardy's Poetry and Short Stories', *Victorian Poetry* 31:1, Spring 1993, pp. 41–60.
Purdy, Richard Little, *Thomas Hardy: A Bibliographical Study* (Oxford: Clarendon Press, [1954] rev. edn, 1968).
Radford, Andrew, 'Thomas Hardy's "The Fiddler of the Reels" and Musical Folklore', *Thomas Hardy Journal* (15:2), May 1999, pp. 72–81.
Ray, Martin, *Thomas Hardy: A Textual Study of the Short Stories* (Aldershot: Ashgate, 1997).
Richardson, Angelique, ' "How I mis-mated myself for love of you!": The Biologization of Romance in Hardy's *A Group of Noble Dames*', *Thomas Hardy Journal* (14:2), May 1998, pp. 59–76.
Ruskin, John, *Notes on Some Principal Pictures Exhibited in the Rooms of the Royal Academy, 1875* (London, 1875).
Scarry, Elaine, 'Work and the Body in Hardy', *Representations* 3, 1983, pp. 90–123.
Schor, Esther, *Bearing the Dead: The British Culture of Mourning from the Enlightenment to Victoria* (Princeton, NJ: Princeton University Press, 1995).
Shaw, Valerie, *The Short Story: A Critical Introduction* (London: Longman, 1983).
Smiles, Samuel, *Self-Help, with Illustrations of Conduct and Perseverance* (London: John Murray, [1859] 1969).
Snell, K. D. M., *Annals of the Labouring Poor: Social Change and Agrarian England, 1660–1900* (Cambridge: Cambridge University Press, 1985).
—, *The Regional Novel in Britain and Ireland, 1800–1990* (Cambridge: Cambridge University Press, 1998).
Stephen, Leslie, *The Life and Letters of Leslie Stephen*, ed. Frederic William Maitland (London: Duckworth, 1906).
Taylor, Richard, *The Neglected Hardy: Thomas Hardy's Lesser Novels* (London: Macmillan, 1982).
Tomalin, Claire, *Thomas Hardy: The Time-Torn Man* (London: Viking, 2006).

Wallace, William, 'New Novels', review of *A Group of Noble Dames*, *The Academy* 40, 1891, p. 153.

Widdowson, Peter, *Hardy in History: A Study in Literary Sociology* (London: Routledge, 1989).

Williams, Raymond, *The Country and the City* (London: Chatto and Windus, 1973).

Wing, George, '*A Group of Noble Dames*: "Statuesque Dynasties of Delightful Wessex"', *Thomas Hardy Journal* (7:2), May 1991, pp. 24–45.

Wotton, George, *Thomas Hardy: Towards a Materialist Criticism* (Goldenbridge, Dublin: Gill and Macmillan, 1985).

Wright, T. R., *Thomas Hardy on Screen* (Cambridge: Cambridge University Press, 2005).

Index

Academy, The, 74, 89
Agricultural depression, 7, 10, 17, 20
Allen, Grant, 69
anagnorisis, 128
ancestors, 6, 7, 70, 81, 82, 86
archaeology, 117–18, 134

Benjamin, Walter, 26, 27, 30, 32
Bentley, John, 25
Bildungsroman, 106
Blackwood's Edinburgh Magazine, 12
Boccaccio, Giovanni, *Decameron*, 61, 89
Boumelha, Penny, 13, 50
Brady, Kristin, 22, 23, 27, 38, 45, 51, 62, 72, 76, 77, 80, 134–5
Brontë, Charlotte, *Jane Eyre*, 42
Browne, Martha, 15, 19
burial, x, 31, 34, 59, 124–6
Bushrod, James, 5

Charles II, 122
Chelsea Hospital pensioners, 25
children, ix, 7, 53, 55–6, 57, 66, 69, 71, 72, 73, 74, 75, 76, 81, 82, 108, 109–10, 113–15
class identity, 60, 61, 67, 69, 81, 82, 83, 96
clichés, 61, 102
Cockerell, Sydney, 28
Covent Garden, 98
Crystal Palace, 108, 109, 130

Dalziel, Pamela, xii
Darcy, Lady Penelope, 85

Darwin, Charles, *The Descent of Man*, 70
dereliction, 126–7
disinterment, 117–18, 124–6, 127, 128
Dickens, Charles, 68
 Great Expectations, 128

Egdon Heath, 8
eugenics, 69–71

femininity, ideology of, 13, 14, 63
Flower, Newman, 17
Fordingbridge, 135
Fox, Stephen, 59, 64–5
free indirect style, 65, 100–1
French Revolution, 120–2

Galton, Sir Francis, *Hereditary Genius*, 69–71
galvanism, 21
gaze, ix, 13, 14, 19, 21, 62, 63, 76, 77
geology, 107, 131
Gilmartin, Sophie, 30
Gittings, Robert, 14, 15, 19
Graphic, viii, 53, 54, 61, 66, 73, 83, 85, 105
Great Exhibition, 25, 107, 109, 110, 131
Greek tragedy, 87, 104, 123, 126
Grey, Lady Jane, 19
Grundyism, viii, 104

hanging, 7, 8, 9, 10, 11, 12, 14, 15, 17, 18, 19, 21
hangman, 7, 8, 9, 10, 11, 12, 16, 18

142 Index

Hardy, Thomas
  his objectivity, 26
  his political views, 10
  his telescopic vision, vii, 1–4
  Works:
  *The Life and Works of Thomas
    Hardy* (ed. Millgate), 2, 3, 4, 5, 8,
    10, 15, 25, 28, 29, 30, 39, 54, 61
  Drama:
  The Dynasts, 24
  Essays:
  'Candour in English Fiction', 104–5,
    115
  'The Dorsetshire Labourer', 19
  'The Profitable Reading of Fiction',
    105, 115
  Novels:
  'Novels of Character and
    Environment', 5, 37
  Far From the Madding Crowd, 3,
    14, 45, 123
  Jude the Obscure, 55, 56, 74
  The Mayor of Casterbridge, 12, 16,
    17, 22, 31, 36, 40, 43, 45, 98
  A Pair of Blue Eyes, 77
  The Poor Man and the Lady, 10, 54
  The Pursuit of the Well-Beloved, 40,
    86, 106
  The Return of the Native, 1, 4, 43,
    46, 105, 116, 118
  Tess of the d'Urbervilles, viii, x, 5,
    31, 35, 40, 54, 55, 57, 60, 65, 70,
    71, 79, 86, 87, 88, 104, 105, 106
  The Trumpet Major, 46, 123
  Two on a Tower, 35, 54–5
  Under the Greenwood Tree, 14, 54,
    79, 108
  The Woodlanders, 31, 40, 43, 56,
    57, 58, 59, 82
  Poetry:
  'Afterwards', 1, 27
  'At Castle Boterel', 4
  'At Middle-Field Gate in February',
    61
  'At Rushy Pond', 58
  'Her Secret', 79
  'Neutral Tones', 58
  'The New Toy', 74
  'Old Furniture', 27

'The Pedigree', 86
Satires of Circumstance, 86
'She Charged Me', 76
Short Stories:
A Changed Man, vii, ix–x, 117, 120,
  124, 130
'A Changed Man', 124, 130–134
'A Committee-Man of "The Terror"'
  120–2
'The Duke's Reappearance', 122–3
'Enter a Dragoon', 124, 127–30
'The Grave by the Handpost', 4, 59,
  124–7
'Master John Horseleigh, Knight',
  119
'A Mere Interlude', 35
'A Tryst at an Ancient Earthwork',
  117–18
A Group of Noble Dames, viii
'Dame the First: The First Countess
  of Wessex', 53, 54, 56–62, 64, 65,
  66, 71, 72, 73, 87
'Dame the Second: Barbara of the
  House of Grebe', 62–7, 68, 79, 90
'Dame the Third: The Marchioness
  of Stonehenge', 55, 66–72, 74, 79
'Dame the Fourth: Lady Mottisfont',
  55, 70, 72–5
'Dame the Fifth: The Lady Icenway',
  72, 76–80, 83
'Dame the Sixth: Squire Petrick's
  Lady', 55, 70, 72, 80–3
'Dame the Seventh: Anna, Lady
  Baxby', 83–5
'Dame the Eighth: The Lady
  Penelope', 54, 85–7
'Dame the Ninth: The Duchess of
  Hamptonshire', 54, 85, 87–8
'Dame the Tenth: The Honourable
  Laura', 85
'Destiny and a Blue Cloak', 41–2, 85
*An Indiscretion in the Life of an
  Heiress and other stories*, xii
'An Indiscretion in the Life of an
  Heiress', 54
Life's Little Ironies, ix, xii, 106, 115,
  130
'The Fiddler of the Reels', 25, 31,
  68, 74, 75, 106–10, 131

'For Conscience' Sake', 94
'An Imaginative Woman', 81–2, 93, 106, 107, 110–15
'On the Western Circuit', ix, 99–104
'The Son's Veto', 32, 95–9
'To Please His Wife', 42, 84
'A Tragedy of Two Ambitions', 93–4, 106
'The Winters and the Palmleys', 17, 18
Wessex Tales, vii, viii, xii, 105
'The Distracted Preacher', 29, 32, 45–9
'Fellow-Townsmen', 5, 21, 26, 31, 35, 36, 82
'Interlopers at the Knap', 7, 31, 40–6, 56, 57, 58, 82
'The Melancholy Hussar of the German Legion', 5, 23, 24, 26, 29, 30–4, 36, 46, 49
'The Three Strangers', 7–11, 49
'A Tradition of Eighteen Hundred and Four', 23–9, 46
'The Withered Arm', 2, 3, 4, 5, 7, 8, 11–23, 26, 40, 49, 62, 63, 87, 128
Harper's Bazaar, 57, 85, 88, 105
Harper's Christmas (annual), 24
Havisham, Miss, 128
home, idea of, 32, 89, 97–8, 99
Homer, *Odyssey*
allusions to Penelope, 95–6
allusions to Telemachus, 96
Hutchins, John, *The History and Antiquities of the County of Dorset*, 59, 60, 82, 83, 84, 85, 86
Hyde Park Corner, 130

Ilchester, Earls of, 60
illiteracy, 18, 96, 99, 104
inheritance, 80, 122
interludes, viii, 34–7, 39, 79, 121, 127

King, Kathryn, xii, 28, 51

Lea, Hermann, 1, 2, 50
legal language, 101
Locker, William, 53, 54

Lodge, David, 1, 50
Longman's Magazine, 19, 85
Lord's cricket ground, 98
Lytton, Lord, 89

Macmillan, 106
Manford, Alan, xii
Marcus Aurelius, 39
marking, on body and landscape, vii, 2–7, 9, 11, 12, 13, 14, 20, 21, 29, 30, 31, 32, 33, 34, 37, 38, 40, 44, 47, 49, 57, 58, 62, 63, 69, 75
marriage, viii–ix, 33, 35–6, 40, 42, 44, 45, 46, 48, 53, 54, 55, 56, 65, 69, 70, 71, 75, 77, 83, 84, 86, 87, 88, 89, 111, 119, 121, 128, 129
marriage market, 42, 43, 44, 45, 46, 56, 57
Melbury Osmond, 60
memorialisation, 31, 34, 64–5, 66, 68, 79, 80
Miller, J. Hillis, 5, 6, 26, 33, 34, 35, 36, 37, 38, 44, 50, 51, 58
Millgate, Michael, xii, 53, 60, 116
Monmouth, Duke of, 122–3
monstrous births, 81
Moule, Rev. Henry, 135
Moynahan, Julian, 134
Munro, Neil, 15
Murray's Magazine, 106
music, 108–9, 124–6

Napoleon, 24, 28
Napoleonic Wars, viii, ix, 23, 24, 25, 28
narrators, 10, 11, 21, 23, 26–33, 37, 57, 61, 65, 66, 67, 68, 72, 73, 75, 78, 83, 84, 87, 88, 89, 90, 103–4, 111, 114, 115, 117–19

Osgood, McIlvaine, 54, 106

parentage, 53, 68, 69, 74, 75, 76, 77, 81, 107, 109–10, 113–15
Peck, John, 123, 135
peripeteia, 128
photography, 21, 22, 23
Pied Piper, 108
Pite, Ralph, 3, 4, 50

present tense, 117–18
Priddle, Nanny, 59, 60
Punch, 57
Pygmalion myth, 66

railway, 109
Ray, Martin, 28, 59, 62, 135
'redundant woman', 42, 45
repetition, 5, 6, 44, 86, 91
Richardson, Angelique, 69, 71
Richardson, Samuel, 68
Rossetti, Dante Gabriel, 'Stillborn Love', 114–15
Ruskin, John, 57
Russell, Lady Anne, 84

Saturday Review, 122
scientific language, 21, 22, 69, 100, 108
Selby, James, 5, 29, 31, 46
sensory perceptions, 30
sexual rivalry, 13, 14, 18, 20, 21, 40–6, 66, 68, 84
Shakespearean tragedy, 104
Shaw, Valerie, 135
Shelley, Percy Bysshe, *Prometheus Unbound*, 114
Sherborne Castle, 84
Sketch, The 14
Sleeping Beauty, 43–4, 89
Smiles, Samuel, *Self-Help*, 82
smuggling, 29, 45–9
Snell, Keith, 17, 115

social inequality, 62, 67, 83, 119
soldiers, ix–x, 32, 33, 71, 72, 123–37
Stephen, Leslie, 21, 23
stereotypes, 102
Strangways-Horner, Elizabeth, 59
Strangways-Horner, Susannah, 59
Strangways-Horner, Thomas, 59
'struggle for existence', 43
Stuart, Mary, 19
surveillance, 99, 130
Swetman, Betty, 60

Teck, Duke and Duchess of, 70
Tomalin, Claire, 116
Trench, Herbert, *Napoleon* (play), 28
Trenchard family, 85

voyeurism, 99, 130

Wallace, William, 74, 89
Waterloo, 126
West Country, vii
Westminster Abbey, x
widowhood, 18, 64, 65, 66, 68, 76, 78, 79, 86, 95, 128, 132
Windle, Bertram, 31
Wordsworth, William, 81
'Woman Question, The', 42
Wotton, George, 13, 50

York Hussars ('Kings German Legion'), 29, 30, 31
Yorkshire, 128